PRESS ON!

Press On!

Michael Hollings
– his life and witness –

Edited by

JOCK DALRYMPLE

JOAN MCCRIMMON

TERRY TASTARD

McCrimmons
Great Wakering, Essex, England

First published in Great Britain in 2001 by
MCCRIMMON PUBLISHING CO. LTD.
10-12 High Street, Great Wakering, Essex, SS3 0EQ
Telephone 01702–218956   Fax 01702–216082
email: mccrimmons@dial.pipex.com
www.mccrimmons.com

ISBN 0-85597-626-8

British Library Cataloguing in Publication Data.
A catalogue record for this book is available from the British Library.

Cover design by Nick Snode
Typeset in Times New Roman 11/14pt and 10/13pt
Printed and bound by Polestar Wheatons, Exeter, Devon

Contents

CHRONOLOGY

Born Camberley	30th December 1921
Coldstream Guards	1941
Awarded MC	1942
Beda College	October 1946
Meets Padre Pio	March 1947
Ordained Rome	8th April 1950
Assistant Priest, St Patrick's, Soho Square	1950-1954
Westminster Cathedral	1954-1958
University Chaplain, London	1958-1959
University Chaplain, Oxford	1959-1970
Parish Priest, St Anselm's, Southall	1970-1978
Parish Priest, St Mary of the Angels, Bayswater	1978-1997
Awarded MBE	1993
Died London	21st February 1997

Introduction

On February 27th, 1997, I met Jock Dalrymple on the stairs of St Mary of the Angels after the first of Michael's two Requiem Masses. Accompanied by the strains of 'Michael row the boat ashore' from the steel band playing outside in the street, the decision was taken together that a book must be written to commemorate the life and work of Michael Hollings.

Neither of us were fully aware then of the enormity of the task we were taking on. Michael's life had been so very full – and as soon as the news became known, offers of help were made from many different sources – fellow clergy, family, friends and parishioners, a group of whom had already begun to collect material on Michael and who generously handed it over to us.

Six months later, in September 1997, while still trying to piece together the jigsaw of the book, I met Terry Tastard at the National Conference of Priests in Birmingham (where some thirty years earlier Michael had first persuaded the Conference to accept a bookstall manned by my publishing house). Terry offered to help in any way he could – a blessing indeed since his gentle but firm editorial thrust has kept everything on course.

We arranged to meet together for the first time in a hotel near Paddington Station, but since it turned out to be under renovation, an alternative venue was found nearby – a tiny café with an overwhelming smell of fish and chips. There *Press On* was born.

The book begins chronologically – the first three chapters, written by Jock, cover Michael's early life, war experiences and seminary formation and conclude with his priestly ordination and appointment to his first parish in Soho in August 1950. Thereafter, apart from the chapters which describe and assess his years at Oxford and in Southall, we adopt a more thematic approach examining Michael the ecumenist, Michael and the open house, Michael, pastor to the sick and the dying, Michael, spreader of the Word and Michael, teacher of prayer. Several are written from very personal perspectives – as seems right since so much of Michael's ministry was personal, one to one. The book concludes with a brief reflection on his final Way of the Cross, with Anthony Baxter's and Cardinal Hume's sermons at his Requiem Masses, and with a bibliography compiled by his friend Joan Cooley.

Inevitably there are gaps – perhaps a future biographer might fill them? But I hope what follows will give every reader a deeper understanding of Michael Hollings, the man, the priest, the counsellor and the friend.

Joan McCrimmon

CHAPTER ONE

Childhood, Adolescence and the War

JOCK DALRYMPLE

Michael Hollings was born on 30th December 1921, in Camberley, the third child of Lt. Commander Richard Hollings, and his wife, Molly. His father's family were Anglican, and according to Michael in *Living Priesthood*, the most autobiographical of his books, 'had built Church of England churches in Yorkshire and refused to have a Roman Catholic in the house.'[1] Richard's mother, Nina, was one of the celebrated Smyth sisters: one, Ethel Smyth, the composer and suffragette, had conducted her political song 'Shoulder to Shoulder' with a toothbrush from her cell in Holloway Jail; another was the wife of Archbishop Randall Davidson of Canterbury; Nina herself was a notable rider to hounds, and in the First World War, having lost a son at the Somme, ran an X-ray unit on the Italian front.

Richard Hollings, however, was not a very prominent figure in Michael's childhood. The absences brought about by a naval career were compounded by an unofficial separation from his wife, and then by tuberculosis. He died in 1928 in Switzerland when Michael was six. In later life he could recall only one encounter with his father.

Richard and Molly Hollings. Married November 1914.

---

[1] *Living Priesthood* (McCrimmons, 1991), p18

Michael

Michael was, therefore, largely brought up by his mother, Molly, the eldest child of Sir Walter and Lady Hamilton-Dalrymple. The Hamilton-Dalrymples were an old Scots family, who had lived in North Berwick since 1694. Their adherence to Catholicism, however, was much more recent, the consequence of Sir Walter's marriage to Alice Mary Clifford, the daughter of a venerable English recusant family. Michael always delighted in the fact that this lineage offered him direct descent from Cardinal Thomas Weld, a widower who was ordained a priest and subsequently appointed Cardinal, enlivening Rome in the 1830's by driving around in his carriage with his grandchildren. Such descent did not, however, guarantee marital stability – Walter left his wife and children, and settled in Alassio in Italy, while Alice Mary moved south to London to escape the ignominy of a separation. She and her unmarried daughter, Marjorie, who lived with her in Egerton Gardens, used to spend every Christmas with the Hollingses.

Richard Hollings' death left Michael in a close-knit family unit of four – with his mother, his brother Tony, and his sister Sylvia – and, as a family, facing increasing financial constraints. In the early 1920's they had moved from a house in Camberley called 'Toft' to another house in the same avenue called 'Stanton', quite close to the fire station of which Nina Hollings had laid the foundation stone. One of Michael's earliest memories was of himself and Tony racing down the street to watch the engines go out to tackle the frequent heath fires near Camberley; of visits to the annual fair next door at Recreation Ground; and of a fascination with cacti, of which he soon had his own impressive collection.

A third move, in 1928, took the family to a new semi-detached house quite near the railway line. However, the main source of income, the family trust, had been invested in government stocks, which suffered greatly because of rampant inflation. As a result they were forced to move once more, choosing Woodstock in Oxfordshire, according to Sylvia, because of an advertisement in the *Universe* about a new parish there which needed support. In Woodstock they rented a Queen Anne house called Ramillies, opposite the Town Hall. The highlight of the family's involvement in church life for Michael and Tony was the chance to show primitive cartoon movies on a hand projector to other children in the school holidays – in between their own family holidays at Littlehampton in Sussex and Salcombe-on-Sea in Devon.

One feature of everyday life was what Tony Hollings described as living in the 'all pervading atmosphere' of the First World War. Being brought up in its aftermath meant that 'not only were we told of near relatives and close friends who died in Flanders Field but we were also willing listeners to our Aunt Marjorie's tales of her work as a VAD (Voluntary Aid Detachment) in France.' Moreover, evidence of the war was all around them: 'Many men on crutches, men with one leg, men with none at all pushing themselves around on little wheeled boards. Men with one or both arms missing, men without noses and so on. It must have had some effect on us all.' Another feature was the influence of Lourdes. Molly and Marjorie were devotees and went every year as handmaids on the National Pilgrimage with the Society of Our Lady of Lourdes. Michael later recalled in an article for the *Universe* how frequently he heard them singing 'Ave, Ave, Ave Maria' to themselves – and 'endless talk and reminiscence about handmaids, brancardiers, baths, processions, blessings, trips to Gavarnie and so on.'

Michael seems, despite his sister's recollection of him as 'an enthusiast for all sorts of games played with enormous energy', to have been a nervous and very shy child, devoted to his mother and to life at home. Certainly the occasional autobiographical glimpses he offers us suggest this. In 1978, in a Radio 3 equivalent to *Desert Island Discs* entitled *Man of Action*, he spoke of one of his earliest musical memories:

Tony, Sylvia and Michael Hollings in 1925

'I was really afraid of the dark as I was the youngest child. I was sent off to bed upstairs, and my mother used to leave me with the door open, with a light on the landing, and the comforting sounds of the family downstairs. But what really made me relax, and feel totally at peace, was when my mother allowed me to go down, and she played the piano for a short while, and every shadow seemed to be absorbed in the music.'

In his book about confession, *Go in Peace* (1976), Michael describes 1920's Catholic sacramental preparation – with an extremely nervous seven-year-old 'being instructed and coached towards my first confession' on Saturday mornings 'in a tin hall which had been the old church before a new stone church was built in front of it.' The classes involved repeating by heart questions and answers out of the current Catechism of Christian Doctrine, and learning the form confession would take. 'I was very shy and timid… I dreaded Saturday mornings and the classes'. More worrying still, though, was the thought of his first confession itself. 'What I had to confess seemed relatively unimportant compared with the fear that I would forget the correct words in the form, or dry up altogether.' In the event, it 'was just as terrifying as I had feared!'

Nor did it seem to get easier,

> especially after the occasion when I went into the dark confessional, having arrived first in church at the time advertised for confessions, and went through all I had to say – only to realise after a long pause that there was no priest at the other side of the grill! I came out red-faced to the grins of the queue which had now formed and the alarming figure of the priest arriving, which meant my return to the box and a repeat of everything… From this young viewpoint, my going to confession and going to the dentist were about equally unpleasant. (2)

Michael was about seven when he had his first direct experience of death – as he later described in an autobiographical passage in *Alive to Death* (1976). The death, however, was not that of a human being but of the family dog.

---

2 *Go in Peace* (McCrimmons, 1990), pp13-14

The dog was run over. Somehow he struggled a considerable distance back home, and when I saw him first, lay panting his life away by the wall of our house. He was only a mongrel but he was real. The gathered family and friends lamented, but did not seem able to do anything except call the vet. What did I feel? Well memory says I felt helpless, because I wasn't allowed to touch him, and everyone was just saying 'Poor thing' and 'What a shame'... and I did not know why the big grown-up world didn't or couldn't do something. I was angry, defeated, heart-broken and filled with a kind of hatred against 'them'. And part of me was mercifully numb so that after a day or two, I was quite OK again.

Poignantly, he also commented: 'It is sad for me, but I am afraid true, that the death of the dog was far more vivid and distressing than the death of my father, both of which occurred as "early memories".' (3)

Given his diffidence, it is not surprising that Michael 'hated with a deep hate' being sent away as an eight-year-old from his very close family life to boarding school at Avisford in Sussex. Avisford was run by a family acquaintance, Charles Jennings, who had been an instructor at Sandhurst, but after two terms Michael was removed from there and sent to another prep school, the Jesuit-run St John's in Egham. This had the slight advantage of 'home being just a short bus ride away,' but he remained miserable. In later years, he remembered himself as a little boy who was 'immensely shy' and 'was never trusted to appear on stage or in a show because I either tripped up in nervousness or broke down and cried.' (4)

At thirteen, Michael won a scholarship to St John's senior school, Beaumont. In *Living Priesthood*, he described how he 'feared and hated' it just as much as he had St John's, Egham. Initially, he continued to be very lacking in confidence: one of the masters, Fr Ronald Moffat SJ, taught him English, Latin, History and RE in his first year, and recalls Michael sitting at the back of the class near the door, 'intensely self-

---

3 *Alive to Death: Thoughts on Suffering, Death & Mourning* (Mayhew-McCrimmon, 1976) p8
4 *Living Priesthood*, p22

16

conscious and blushing to the roots of his hair' (5) whenever he was asked a question. However, he did slowly begin to develop and mature. Reflecting on his schooling he commented: 'I can see in hindsight it did me good' – 'the strict Jesuit discipline gave me something, much as I disliked it', while 'I made friendships some of which have lasted to this day, not only among the boys but among the Jesuits and lay staff.' (6) One close and lasting friend was John Corbould, the son of a convert Anglican clergyman, while Fr Moffat himself proved an enduring influence. 'In his wisdom, he took four of us who were somehow "oddbods" and gave us a "year off" at fifteen when we were left free to read widely, study with some intensity on limited subjects in a group, and work on a tutorial basis.' (7) From Fr Moffat, Michael felt he learnt something he was grateful for throughout his life and which he always encouraged others to imitate – the desire and capacity to read a book whenever the opportunity presented itself.

In his second year at Beaumont, in 1936, there was an early indication of Michael's writing gifts. He won a newspaper competition in which he had to give reasons why he should attend the Coronation as a spectator and was awarded a seat at Regent's Park as a prize. Unfortunately, however, he succumbed to measles and was unable to go.

Around this time, when Michael was a young teenager, he had another brush with death, the consequence of a car crash.

> My mother and sister were both concussed, I was all right, but an old man in the front seat was badly hurt. That night I was alone at home with my mother and sister, both of whom were shocked and not too well. I was in torment that night, and in a way alone, fearing for my mother and sister, and dreading that the older man might die. I felt 'dirty' somehow and 'responsible', and angry, especially when the man did die, despite all my prayers. (8)

---

5 Interview conducted by Alasdair Black, 1992
6 *Living Priesthood*, pp18-19
7 Ibid, p18
8 *Alive to Death*, p9

For someone so sensitive, confession as a teenager was especially diffi-cult. 'I was at boarding school, Mass and Holy Communion were every day, confession was expected to be every week or so, and a sharp eye was kept to make sure we came to Mass and Holy Communion each day unless we were sick. I got through these years painfully and under tension' – although, as he adds, 'this was not simply centred on confession.' (9)

Fr Moffat, interviewed in the early 1990's, remembered Michael in his final years at Beaumont as tall and slight, with red cheeks and dark beau-tifully parted hair; he was always tidy and well turned out, a neatness which also showed itself in his written work. He recalled him as 'well-behaved and well-mannered' – 'one had the impression of a sensitive, intelligent, quiet person, with a great deal in reserve, waiting for other cir-cumstances in which to develop.' (10)

In 1939 war broke out. Michael's brother, Tony, had joined the navy in 1937, and his sister, Sylvia, now joined the WRAF. Michael himself persuaded his mother, who was already ill with the cancer that would eventually kill her, that it would be a waste of money for him to go back to school for a further year. Instead, he caught a bus into Oxford and asked how he could get into the University. He was sent to St Catherine's Non-Collegiate Society where they agreed to

Michael as an undergraduate

take him – 'all in one morning, without any exam or anything.' His expe-rience of life over the next two years, 'varied from cooking and cleaning and gardening for my mother, to wining and dining in college; from train-ing by day in the Army Training Corps, to attending pacifist meetings in the evening; from going to Mass and working with the Catholic Chaplaincy groups to endless socialist and Marxist meetings in college rooms and odd pubs.' (11)

9 *Go in Peace*, pp14-15
10 Interview with Alasdair Black
11 *Living Priesthood*, pp18-19

In *Man of Action* Michael offered a slightly different perspective on those years: 'My schooling was pre World War II. We were not penniless, but poor' – within a certain social framework –

> and I can't remember ever having gone to a concert until I arrived at Oxford as an undergraduate, just after the war had broken out. There I tried to pick up the culture I felt I did not have before. In school, I had always been told I was tone-deaf, but I certainly knew what I liked, and Oxford was a place for concerts. There, despite war, I revelled in the complex existence of training corps and pacifist meetings, politics and religion, history, which I was reading, and the arts. I loved the 18th century and the 19th century in history, but loved them through Beethoven, Bach, Mozart, Brahms and Elgar in music, and through Goldsmith, Swift, Horace Walpole, Kingsley, Dickens and Disraeli in literature.

Throughout this exhilarating time he was able to live at home. His first cousin, Elsie Gibbs, who was working in the War Office at Blenheim, recalls how kind Molly and Michael were to her – 'they were such fun to be with... we went to cinemas in the evening and had delicious suppers.' It was the last occasion he would live with his mother for any length of time, although her influence remained strongly with him throughout his life. In *Living Priesthood*, he wrote: 'I will always consider myself fortunate to have had the background experience of a home where we were expected to play our part in working in the house, cleaning, cooking etc, as well as being made aware of others outside who had far less than we did. My mother was a great sharer; we picked up some of that from her.'(12) And in *Day by Day*, he answered the question 'why do I pray?' with 'Because my mother prayed', – 'she was a woman who prayed deeply, believed deeply and lived out her belief in God and man by the love which flowed from her, especially to those poorer than herself.' (13)

Michael's friendship with John Corbould, who had also gone up to Oxford from Beaumont, continued to develop. John's younger brother Michael (Dom Edward Corbould, OSB, of Ampleforth Abbey) recalls

---

12 *Living Priesthood*, p226
13 *Day by Day*, (Mayhew-McCrimmon, 1972), p10

how Michael used to come to stay with the family at Dilham in Norfolk from 1939 onwards – and how central his faith was even then.

> He was always cheerful and enormously kind to us younger children, but there was an underlying reserve and seriousness. Being in an isolated part of Norfolk we were five miles from the nearest market town, North Walsham, which did in fact have a Catholic Church. My father and mother were converts to Catholicism in the early 1930's and my father went to Mass daily without fail, usually taking one or two members of the family with him. When Michael came to stay he would always join my father in the early morning journey into North Walsham. During the war with petrol rationing this would frequently necessitate taking to a bicycle, but this never deterred Michael. Obviously his wartime visits after 1941 were determined by his period of leave.

Michael had joined the Home Guard early in the war – and had his first experience of real fear during the Blitz in London, when he helped in warden work in the air raid shelters. In 1941, he was called up. Tony Hollings remembers Michael's description of the interview arranged for him by the leader of the Oxford OTC (Officers' Training Corps) with a Coldstream Guards Colonel in Birdcage Walk, London. It consisted of three questions: 'Do you hunt? Do you shoot? Do you fish?' Michael answered no to all three, but was still sent to Sandhurst and commissioned.

Sylvia (WRAF), Michael (Home Guard), Tony (RN), 1940

Soon he was 'strutting round on King's Guard at Buckingham Palace', after which he 'got the worst ever report from an assault course in Scotland, where the Commanding Officer said I should not have been commissioned as I lacked guts and had no powers of leadership.' (14)

---

14 *Living Priesthood*, p19

The next four years, most of which Michael spent in Africa and Italy, tell a different story, although it is not one recounted in detail in *Living Priesthood* which offers a mere half paragraph on this period.

> Overseas service was thrilling, terrifying, boring and enormously maturing. God went out of my life. People came in. They were real and so was life. I had to face myself and know that I was a coward in front of danger, that I hated hardship, that I was selfish, but I immensely enjoyed friends and parties and being alive. I wanted so much to stave off facing a battle-weary self and battle-weary companions, the harm and indignity of men broken by shellshock and sheer terror. Oddly God did not come in here – just some kind of basic human instinct and concern. (15)

However, there does survive from that time both Michael's youthful journal, describing his experiences as they occurred in North Africa in 1942 and 1943, and five letters, written to his mother from Italy in 1944. They reveal quite how formative these years were in moulding his personality and influencing the direction his life would take.

The journal opens in December 1942 just after Michael's battalion had gone to North Africa as part of the First Guards Brigade. It begins with a description of how in 'the growing heat of the morning sun, a long line of weary men, walking in single file along the muddy verge of the road on either side, wound over a rise and saw ahead of them, for the first time, the little town and railway station of Medjez-el-Bab.'

Very soon, news reached them of a tank battle further south, followed by an aircraft alert which sent them scuttling for the cover of the trees.

> The usual chorus of 'Spitfire' was followed by the hostile whine of a diving plane. At once we broke all training rules about keeping the white face covered; everyone was looking up, craning to get a better view. Glancing towards the hills, I saw two planes, Messerschmitts they seemed, diving for the road. As I watched, a queer sensation gripped me in the stomach, and my mouth dried up. Falling from beneath the planes and clearly outlined against the sky, were two bombs...

---

15 Ibid, p19

Having survived that, Michael was faced a few days later by the battle of Longstop Hill. On December 22nd, the Battalion – in which Michael was Platoon Commander – made the first of its assaults on the Hill as part of what turned out to be an abortive allied rush for Tunis. Michael's account of how he was wounded in the neck, during a night attack on German positions covered by anti personnel mines, begins somewhat blandly: 'I was silly enough to put my head up at the wrong moment, and the bullet I got in my neck for my troubles, put me out of the next three days of battle.' However, rather than seek treatment immediately, he marched his platoon for several miles: initially, 'progress was slow and my pain in the neck hampered us a bit', but eventually the platoon took their objective, 'in true British fashion, charging with bayonets and shouts on an enemy who had run away', before returning to Medjez. At this point, Michael finally approached a doctor, who examined him with the aid of a candle and asked 'Can you feel anything in your throat, anything unusual?' 'Personally it felt as though there was no front to my throat at all, and at the back there was about an 8mm solid shell jammed near my tongue. It was not worth saying so, and instead I got out "I think there is something stuck there" – It was a pretty obvious remark, considering that there was only one hole, and if something had gone in, as indeed it had, it must still be there.'

Eventually, he was taken off to hospital in an ambulance, where an orderly demanded all his kit and weapons. 'Well, you can't have my pistol, binoculars or fighting knife', retorted Michael. 'If you want anything else take this,' and he drew a primed 36 grenade from his breast pocket.

Shortly afterwards, the surgeon, 'a good and clever man', came in from the operating theatre, had a look at the wound, and said he couldn't offer any hope of getting to work on him till the evening. Michael's journal's account concludes, 'it didn't matter, I was glad to rest'.

Many years later, in *Alive to Death*, Michael expanded slightly on this part of the account, describing how after the ambulance ride, he 'lay on the floor of some farmhouse for what seemed like days, numb, fearful, listless, drifting and terribly sore. Just before I was taken to be operated on, an orderly bent over me: "D'you know so-and-so?" he said, "wounded just where you are. Just died y'know." ' (16)

Two other accounts also survive and paint a rather fuller picture of the incident. The citation for the Military Cross that Michael was subsequently awarded for a 'devotion to duty' that 'will be long remembered in his battalion' reads thus:

2nd Lt. Michael Hollings, just after his commissioning, 1942.

> During the whole engagement, as on all previous occasions, this officer showed outstanding powers of leadership. Towards the end of the fighting he was shot through the throat but made no effort to obtain medical treatment and continued to carry out his duties until, as part of the plan of action, he had disengaged his Platoon from the enemy. The Platoon then had to march for some miles, during which time he kept insisting that his injury was of no consequence. When later he reported to the Regimental Aid Post and was evacuated, it was found that his wound was of the gravest nature and must have caused him great pain for many hours. A major operation was at once necessary to save his life.

Forty-five years later, three weeks after Michael's death in February 1997, his sister Sylvia received a letter from Professor Harold Rodgers of Edgbaston, Birmingham, which offered a second perspective on the incident.

> I read in the *Times* the obituary of your brother Michael, and I wondered if he was the brave officer in the 2nd Battalion, the Coldstream Guards, I had as a patient when I was the surgeon of a field surgical unit in North Africa in December 1942. The Coldstreams were engaged in an action a little south of a small town called Medjez-el-Bal. At the end of the action, three wounded men were brought into our medical unit. A lieutenant was the first I examined. He had a wound in the neck. The bullet entering on the right side just below the jaw and traversed the neck. He was bleeding into his mouth and choking as he spat out blood

---

16 *Alive to Death*, pp9-10

clots. As I finished my examination, he spoke with difficulty, saying, 'Doc, would you take the men first?'

I then examined his sergeant who was shot through the femur of the right leg. He also had lost a lot of blood but was in a stable state. When I finished my examination, he said, 'would you take Mr Hollis first, sir?'

The third was a guardsman who had a through and through wound of his leg below the knee with a shattered tibia. He said, 'Permission to speak sir'. I said 'Yes', and he also said 'would you please take Mr Hollis first, sir?' I was so impressed by these three men and this unselfishness, that I made a short speech to them standing at the foot of the stretchers. I said, 'you are the three finest men I have had the honour to operate on. I will have to take you in the order of the seriousness of your wounds and if I don't take Mr Hollis right away, he might die. So I will take him first.' They all came through their operations and were evacuated to a hospital in the rear, I think the next day.

This happened a day or two before Christmas 1942. The name Hollis was from memory and it might well have been Hollings. I wonder if you could let me know if he could possibly have been your brother... I have often recounted his story as an example of bravery and unselfishness.

Nor was that the end of Michael's involvement in the campaign. His contemporary from both Beaumont and the Coldstream Guards, Sir Reginald Secondé, recalled in his obituary of Michael in the *Guards Magazine* how, characteristically, he had 'caught his battalion by surprise shortly afterwards, when he turned up with a fat bandage around his neck having dismissed himself from hospital and hitchhiked his way by military transport to the front', and how he had continued to prove himself 'an officer of coolness and courage.' Eventually, Michael did return to England on sick leave. During his time in North Africa he had corresponded with his old schoolmaster, Fr Moffat, who noted the extent to which Michael's writing style had improved from his schooldays. But he was impressed by more than the style. 'They were the considerable letters of a somebody, not merely sketches.' (17)

Two questions remain unresolved about Michael and his wartime experiences. The first concerns how he occupied himself while stationed in London or on leave there; the second, and more important, is whether he lost faith in God – as he frequently later asserted he had – and if so, exactly when.

In *Living Priesthood*, Michael wrote of how at Oxford, he had 'attended the first really secular society of my lifetime', where he 'discovered ideas and situations which shook me, even given what I had come across in various ways in school days.' However, 'the most different and sophisticated arena into which I suddenly found myself pitched was the London life of a young Guards Officer in wartime... the proximity of bombing and the expectancy of a short London posting before going overseas to fight, opened the way to a riotous kind of life for anyone who fancied it.'

Michael went on to reflect how he was 'not properly of the Guards background'. This was in contrast to most of his fellow officers who

> seemed to be of well-heeled families from famous public schools who already knew their way round London. I was a 'country bumpkin', in that respect; and also a very poor one. I had only my pay. They were kindness itself; I had known many of my fellow officers vaguely at Oxford and better at Sandhurst. They showed me round London nightlife, introducing me to a night-club existence filled with wine, women and song, which often had us literally staggering onto parade the following morning.

> It was a strange life of irresponsibility, with little or no belief in God... an experience of 'eat, drink and be merry for tomorrow we die'.

That passage refers mainly to the time between Michael's commissioning in the Coldstream Guards in 1941 and his departure to North Africa in November 1942. But it also 'extended in a lesser way to the few-and-far-between leave periods which we subsequently had during the fighting in North Africa and Italy'. [18] However, by then he was showing the more

---

[18] *Living Priesthood*, p61

serious and compassionate side of his nature. Edward Corbould, for example, remembers him fitting in a brief visit to Dilham, but that 'most of his leave was spent visiting relatives of those in his battalion who had been killed.'

In early 1944, Michael was back in action, this time in Italy. From there, he often wrote home to his mother, by now seriously ill. Five letters from the first four months survive, offering a gruesome and vivid picture of that campaign, as well as illustrating the closeness and tenderness of his relationship with her, and his own passionate nature. They also suggest that as late as June 1944, God had not gone out of his life.
On February 13th, he is writing from Monte Ornito, in the south of the peninsula:

> Darling... Conditions out here were, I believe, described by the Russian Military Mission as far exceeding in frightfulness anything that happens in the Soviet War. I can well believe it in the mountains – I am now writing from about 3,000 feet up – there are no roads or even tracks... at night it is so cold you could hardly believe it to be true... for three days our clothes were wet – this led to an amazing performance, when our blankets and greatcoats, trousers etc froze stiff as a board...
> ...Darling, it is so appalling the way our friends get killed and wounded. How costly and hateful it is. The worst blow I have suffered is the loss of Teddy Hughes. ... I helped to get him onto a stretcher. He was hit in the legs and stomach but still conscious. When he recognised me, he said "Mike" in such a touching way. I very nearly cried. So I squeezed his hand and gave him some morphia. I had to go and do some fighting, so that was the last I saw of him... poor Teddy, may he live through it. I would be very grateful if you would write to his mother – Mrs. M. Hughes, 200 Albert Road, Sheffield, and tell her what I have told you.
> Pray hard for me, Darling. We have George [Dom George Forbes, OSB, a monk of the Benedictine Abbey of Ampleforth and chaplain to the Coldstream Guards] with us and he is splendid.* Tonight we have a little

---

* Dom George Forbes was awarded the MC at Monte Ornito. At the end of the citation describing Fr George's bravery, the commanding officer, Lt Col N. R. Norman writes, 'He was an inspiration to the whole Battalion, and I am not skilled enough with a pen adequately to describe his conduct.'

service at 8 o'clock. This is the hardest life I have ever lived, we are so cold we shiver at all times, day and night, and when we are not shivering with cold, we shiver with fright... I love you very much, Darling. I love all at home. Pray that God may be merciful to us in this bloodshed...

Nine days later, things are no easier:

...I would rather go through two African campaigns, than have ever again a fortnight like the last. It was the hardest, most testing, coldest, most exciting, harrowing, most terrifying, physically exhausting and mentally exacting that any man could, in my estimation, be asked to perform. I naturally cannot tell you how many casualties we suffered, but we sustained six very determined counter-attacks and captured in that period about 200 prisoners...

...We climbed these hills carrying an immense weight, which almost killed me. One or two fell by the wayside from sheer exhaustion. When we got to the top we had to drive some Germans out and then it rained till we were wet through. We dug all night and moved next day a little higher up. I was with the machine guns while this was happening... the following day we were attacked. I got the guns into position and then went off to help Number 3 Company who had lost their officers. We drove out the Germans in a snowstorm, making prisoners and killing a number... it rained and snowed all night and we lay shivering, drenched through our greatcoats to the skin...

This assault may well have been the bayonet charge mentioned in the Regimental History of the Coldstream Guards, where reference is made to Michael successfully clearing a ridge and taking prisoners.

The letter also contains an allusion to what seems an early attempt at finding a larger audience for his writing: 'I had a letter from Helena saying she could give me an introduction to Murray or Blackwood. That is the way to do it, though of course we would have to get permission from RHQ. It is perfectly all right to get it published if they say "Yes".'

He concludes: 'I hope to go and see Teddy Hughes in a day or two. I have written to his mother. He had both legs broken but was in very good heart and getting on well. He should go back to England.'

27

Two days on, and Michael is suffering further discomfort.

> ...while I was up in the mountains, I had the most huge abscess from a tooth in my lower jaw. I can assure you that it was not pleasant, but it did have the benefit of keeping me awake at night when I might have gone to sleep. On return, I had insomnia of all ridiculous things, probably through being overdone. And now, to crown it all, I have developed an enormous and vastly painful carbuncle on the back of my neck. I have seldom met a more uncomfortable complaint... I am expecting that I shall not go into action next time, as I have been into every battle the Battalion has had, and we always leave some people behind each time...

He also reveals a somewhat 'insurance policy' approach to faith and salvation – '...I went to Mass on Tuesday, and yesterday – Ash Wednesday, I made my Easter duties, so that I am well up-to-date should anything happen...' – before describing how 'in the afternoon I went over to the hospital again and took some more cigarettes, sweets etc. to the men and officers there. They are very patient and brave, but I know so well how awful the whole thing is. Unfortunately I have come to the conclusion that sooner or later, everyone will be hit. It is a matter of how seriously this happens.'

He continues in a way which would not have impressed the later Michael of multiracial Southall and Bayswater. 'On the whole I like Italy far more than Africa. There are churches and chapels at every turn, and though the people are not outwardly much better off or more civilised than the Wogs, they are Europeans and actually merely poor and not uncivilised.' It also perhaps provides a context for the passage in *Living Priesthood* when he reflects on how 'deep down, as a legacy of colonialism and empire, many in the islands [of Great Britain and Ireland] have lived with an almost unconscious sense of superiority over black, brown and yellow. Somehow no one was quite equal to us and we came to consider 'coloured' people as 'uncivilised' or even as more animal than human.'[18] In passing, he also describes the destruction of the Abbey of

18 *Living Priesthood*, p61

Monte Cassino, founded by St Benedict himself in the sixth century. 'We watched the destruction of George Forbes' mother house from a mountain. It was a strange sad sight and not to be forgotten.'

The letter ends: 'I think often of you all and pray I may come back to you... keep praying, writing, and sending me books. I have just had your parcel containing two Dorothy Sayers...'

Three days later, February 27th, he is writing again, this time in apologetic vein:

> I am sorry that I always seem to write you the most depressing of letters, but you are my safety valve, and I cannot help feeling that no one realises the appalling things which happen out here.
> ... I am having a really horrid time with the carbuncle on the back of my neck. I cannot see it, but I am told that it is enormous and like one of those awful sores you see on cattle... I must pray I do not get another one like it, as that would be the end...

With hindsight, the next two paragraphs offer significant pointers to his future calling.

> I am having a very quiet time here, reading and writing letters, as I do not feel much up to anything else... I generally go over to the hospital every few days to take them anything I can get hold of, as I know what this means. Many of them are getting on well and moving to other places, but the nucleus remain who will be weeks and months.
> Father George remains with us. He was wonderful in action, being praised by all. He used to wander about up to the forward companies in the heavier shellfire and action, quite unarmed, and with his funny old stiff cap on – quite alone and quite unperturbed... He was an inspiration to us all and especially to me. Now he says Mass daily and I manage Communion at least each morning which is a blessing.

It was not totally unremitting, however, as he recalled in *Man of Action*. One day,

> suddenly and unexpectedly, two things happened; Vesuvius erupted and I was told to leave the front line for 24 hours. From our hillside perch, the eruption of Vesuvius looked like Naples being bombed but was

very different in close-up, terrifying and hugely powerful. But even more incredible to me was that, as I drove from the Front to Naples, I spent the evening at the opera, listening to Mascagni's *Cavallera Rusticana*.

The next letter to survive is dated 13th June, three and a half months later, and is written from the outskirts of Rome.

...I must apologise for being so long in writing. My last letter was a week ago on the outskirts of Rome. Since then we have had no opportunity of going to the city. I have only seen the dome of St Peter's and the Tiber north of it. The day will come, however. We carry on to the top of Italy, going gladly because it is the nearest way to home. The news is terrific on all sides. Despite the success, there are losses and small failures. We, for instance, have just undergone one of the most terrifying and pitiable battles that can be imagined.

The German is now fighting in the middle of his supply dumps. He has to go back. But rather than leave anything he will fire it all off before he goes. He did this to us the other day. We lay in the bed of a stream. He put two shots ahead, two behind and then the fun began. He hit my carrier and it went up in flames. All I had was burnt in it – bedding, clothing, glasses, map, food... we could do nothing but lie there. The explosions were so close that the force pressed against us each time, like a blow behind the ear. On my left, my driver was hit in the back of the neck... on the right, ten yards away, the Company Commander, his driver and signaller were all hit by the same shells. We alone survived. In a lull we got them away and moved from the area of the burning vehicle. My signaller never reached our destination. A few minutes later we were quiet and I went back to find him. He had been badly hit in the head. I got a shell dressing and a Sergeant to help me... As we were bandaging him up, they began again... as we crawled away a shell burst behind. The Sergeant was killed, but I got away. Eventually I spent the night in a Sherman tank, answering messages over the wireless... soaked to the skin from lying in the stream.

Before all this horror... a rather amusing incident occurred. I was going along the road behind some tanks. We came to a blown bridge... so I was asked by the Squadron Leader to take some men up the hill and cover him until the companies came up. I gaily set off, and climbed the

30

hill with six men, not expecting any excitement. As I came to the top, I turned round to the men behind me and said I thought there might be some new potatoes in the garden. I then looked round and bless me if there wasn't a German lying in position behind a haystack, looking the other way.

I said 'Hand, Hock'. He was even more surprised than I was and came quietly. I then heard noises in the house and made him walk over and tell the others to come out. He shouted to them, but they escaped round a corner while I was watching him. I took a pot shot at them, with a Tommy gun – and missed the three of them. However, we kept the one and he gave us useful information. The Commanding Officer and Adjutant were both wounded and as a result I am for the moment Captain and Adjutant of this Battalion. It is rather a strain to start with but I will settle down I hope. Pray that all may go well, I have just been to Mass to say 'thank you' for being alive…

And he adds a postscript: 'The account sounds as though the Germans had the upper hand, but in fact we pushed on and did the job we were meant to.'

We also have descriptions of Michael the soldier from two of his fellow officers – although from the perspective of half a century later. One, his former school contemporary, Reginald Secondé, wrote in his obituary of how he 'was good company and was liked and admired by all ranks, despite his rather caustic wit. He had a way, when amused, of growing scarlet in the face and shaking with silent laughter. He was also efficient… even drill sergeants would quail at the whiplash of his tongue!'

The other, Sir Ian Fraser, [19] gives us an insight into the second half of the Italian campaign later that year, as well as a fuller description of Michael as a young adjutant. Fraser had been 'lent' by the Scots Guards to the Coldstreamers because they had run out of reinforcements, and had just been appointed junior platoon commander, when he reported for duty

---

19 Sir Ian Fraser, CBE, MC, went on to become a prominent businessman in the City of London – and chairman of Lazard Brothers, Rolls Royce Motors and many other companies.

to Michael 'in a hideous new Florentine castello, San Mezzano', in the Upper Arno valley.

He remembers him at this meeting as 'a slim man of middle height, with a surprisingly rubicund complexion and an engaging, if somewhat shy, smile.' After a quick tour of the house, Michael informed him that, however comfortable it was, they would all have to leave it to pursue the Germans into the foothills of the Apennines. 'He also told me that the Regimental Chaplain was, exceptionally, a Holy Roman called Major George Forbes – I probably knew him from Ampleforth. My documents, which of course he had seen, had stated that I entered the army by way of the Ampleforth College Officer Training Corps. I only learned later that Hollings was also a Catholic and had been educated at Beaumont.'

Fraser was greatly impressed by Michael, the Adjutant, by Forbes, the Chaplain, and by their Commanding Officer, Bob Coates.

> The Adjutant, always a captain, was the man who translated the decisions of the Commanding Officer into verbal and written instructions to the six Company Commanders and others like the doctor, the chaplain and the various camp followers who looked after our physical and spiritual needs. In other words he was the battalion staff officer. The Commanding Officer was a Yorkshire squire called Bob Coates – a wonderful man to serve under. Both Coates and Hollings were well endowed with the gifts most needed by regimental officers – understanding, decisiveness, clarity and – most important of all – leadership.

One of Michael's responsibilities was to maintain discipline among the junior officers, although, according to Fraser, 'he did not believe in asserting too much discipline among us on the rare occasions when we were pulled out of the line and were able to dine together in a mess tent or borrowed castello.' Significantly, his lasting memory of Michael at this time is of the work he shared with George Forbes.

> When the war turned nasty again, and we found ourselves slogging our way through the Northern Apennines on the road to Bologna against furious German resistance, aided by rain, mud and snow, everyone – officers and men – remarked on the help and comfort which they

received from the Adjutant and Regimental Chaplain. I remember many occasions on which Michael or George crept up to the forward positions, frequently under heavy fire, to find out how the lads were getting on. This was the sort of thing which guardsmen remembered and frequently mentioned in their letters home.

Indeed, Michael had prepared himself well for this task of supporting and encouraging his troops. In *Living Priesthood*, he recalled – in the context of the need for serious consideration to be given to the relationship between the role of the priest and that of the psychologist and psychiatrist – how his interest in this whole area had grown out of the 'long sessions in Italy trying to work out with our medical officer the way we could help officers and guardsmen who were being gnawed with fear and becoming quite "bomb-happy".'[20] Elsewhere, he expanded on how once he returned to active service, he was

> fairly constantly in danger… I kept having people killed beside me, or missed death by a few feet. I got nervy, cowardly and afraid. I hated and dreaded going to the front line. I kept down. I had to force myself out, so that I was not for ever too frightened to move on. My own experience made me protective of the men and their lives. I suffered for them, as well as myself and tried hard to help the wounded and the dying, and also those whose nerves got frayed or broken. It was a horrible period and experience. [21]

In the light of all this it is understandable that, later, Coates' successor, Colonel Roddy Hill, visited Dunbar to inspect the OCTU (Officer Cadet Training Unit), he borrowed an army car and drove ten miles specifically to communicate to Michael's uncle, Hew Dalrymple, quite how well respected Michael had become as Adjutant.

Towards the end of the Italian campaign, Michael's mother wrote telling him that she had not long to live and asking him if he could get home. In one of his books on bereavement, *Dying to Live*, he described what happened next:

---

20 *Living Priesthood*, p134
21 *Alive to Death*, p10

> Owing to large casualties we were having an amalgamation of two bat-
> talions at that time. I was among those due to go home – until my opposite
> number who was due to stay took me to one side. He told me he was in his
> forties (I was about twenty-two) and that he had a wife and four children in
> England. Could he go home instead of me? I had to say 'yes' to that. (22)

This 'yes' had not come easily: elsewhere he commented on how this
decision 'took me a good bit of struggling, both through fear and through
longing to get to my mother, but eventually I agreed to stay. I think that
decision did something to me.' (23)

Michael did finally manage to get to see her – but only by volunteering
from Italy to form part of an invasion force for Japan. As he explained
many years later, this 'was not because I wanted to go and fight the
Japanese.' Rather it was because 'my mother was dying of cancer... and
the army would not allow me home.' (24) By volunteering, he was allowed
to return to England.

On his arrival, he went straight to see Molly, finding her 'thin, tired, in
pain but full of joy that I was home. She knew she was incurable, but
went on fighting. We had a horrific time as we had no home and she
stayed for a time in a hotel.' Eventually he and his sister, Sylvia, found a
friendly nursing home for her – but because of his military responsibilities Michael could only visit every few weeks 'to sit with her, to be silent,
and to care for her when she was in pain or vomiting.'

Even that was soon denied him, the army posting him to Palestine not
Japan. 'I had the sorrow of leaving her dying – I was summoned by cable
from Palestine, but was not allowed home. She died without my seeing her
again.' (25)

He was heartbroken: 'I had the pain of lonely distance in Haifa and I
don't mind confessing that I cried myself to sleep in my tent on several

---

22 *Dying to Live* (McCrimmons, 1991), p30
23 *Alive to Death*, p10
24 *Reflections through the Church's Year – Year A* (McCrimmons, 1995), p95
25 *Dying to Live*, p30

nights.' After all his close encounters with violent death in the previous two years, he experienced 'the chaos of emptiness and powerlessness' (26) at a deeper level than ever before.

Did this emptiness and powerlessness coincide with a loss of faith – or was it the beginning of its rediscovery? The evidence is conflicting. In Michael's letters home to his mother we see him as a daily communicant in February 1944, and as going to Mass in June 1944 to say thank you for still being alive. However his later recollections paint a different picture; often in both written and spoken word, he referred back to this period as one of agnosticism. For example, in *Man of Action* talking about the day when Vesuvius erupted and he had slipped away to Naples to *Cavallera Rusticana*, he asserted 'I had at this point in the war lost belief in God, and it took a long time to be rekindled in me. I was put off by Rome, and much of what I saw of the Catholic Church in Italy. I was undermined by war, and by the destruction and futility of what we were at.' Similarly, he wrote in *Day by Day* how 'World War II had an immense effect on me. I "fought" through it, loved the companionship and hated the killing; was shattered, disillusioned, lost sight and sound of God, worked only for my fellow men and not for the cause of war, knew what cowardice was in myself, felt my own emptiness and inability to give anyone anything.'

All this 'led to the end of the war and that in turn to further disillusion'.(27) Not only was he trying to cope with his bereavement far from home, but he was 'engaged in the unpleasant police duties of the Army in the emerging situation of Israel being born out of Palestine.' (28) The year that followed was the decisive turning-point in Michael's life. The intense grieving for his mother 'had the effect of crystallising God's rediscovery of me as I tried to reassess myself and life after war, after her death, and faced by the problems of all the men under my command, many of whom were even more lost than I was.' (29)

---

26 *Alive to Death*, p11
27 *Day by Day*, p11
28 *Man of Action* (Tape)
29 *Alive to Death*, p11

He had but one driving desire at this time – to work for these men and their families. However,

> the more I tried, the more inadequate I realised myself to be... faced with my post-war life, the futility of killing, the joy of other human beings, the very real and immediate and often intimate concerns of these fellow-men of mine... what was the 'how' of my living to be? Quite simply, in statement but not so simply in fact, I needed God, and I needed contact with him, so I found my way through again to belief and to prayer. (30)

As he wrote elsewhere: 'a period of my life came to an end. Some of me died. I had a bout of crippling sinus trouble, plenty of time to think, and the crisis of defence duties in a country developing from Palestine to Israel. It brought me to opt for God... and to decide to try to be a priest.'(31) Indeed, within 18 months of his mother's death, Michael was studying for the priesthood in Rome.

What happened to effect this transformation? Michael never revealed exactly how and when his faith came alive again, but in *Man of Action* he spoke of how 'the plight of the Jews, the walking in Christ's footsteps, and the time to reflect all contributed to a return to belief.'

An initiative Michael took at this time was the introduction of a Battalion newsletter, which he wrote and edited. In one edition he commented on the lack of peace between the Jews and Arabs, and compared it to the way he and his fellow soldiers quarrelled among themselves. He was subsequently very moved by the note of encouragement he received from one of his guardsmen: 'Hope on, hope ever, that friend and brother will love one another. Hope on, hope ever.' (32)

In time, he did indeed discover this hope, and faith too – primarily it seems through the chance the year in Palestine offered him both to walk in Christ's footsteps and to reflect on his wartime experiences in the light

---

30 *Day by Day*, p12
31 *Alive to Death*, p11
32 *Reflections through the Church's Year – Year A*, p79

of that opportunity. As the year went on, Michael 'began to try to visit the various places as the appropriate Gospel or feast day arrived in the Church's calendar.' Soon this became for him 'not only a fascinating attempt at reconstruction but also a most useful source of meditation.' (33)

Chapter 13 and Chapter 14 of Michael's first book, *Hey, You!* (1955), are a remarkably vivid account of these wanderings and, by implication, of Michael's gradual rediscovery of faith. The stated aim of these chapters was to focus on the geography of Palestine and the 'psychology' of the country in order to enter more deeply into the experience of Jesus' Passion. Chapter 13 begins in Galilee where

in the rare morning light you can see the Gospel live; afar off Tabor rises like a carbuncle on a man's face. But it is not this which takes your breath away. Rather it is the brilliant cloud, its edges tinged with gold, which drapes the summit, so that unconsciously you find yourself quoting: 'And as he was yet speaking, behold a bright cloud overshadowed them and lo! a voice out of the cloud saying: This is my beloved Son in whom I am well pleased. Hear ye him.'

And then if you climb the precipitous winding path to the top, the Franciscans will give you a glass of cool red wine, and allow you to walk under the growing heat of the sun, in the rosemary scented garden, in and out among the shady olive trees...

...But you cannot linger, for not far away little Nazareth calls you. Surely it is the most captivating of towns, set in the hills high above the plain; I felt certain each time I went up to Nazareth that, despite the rejection, Our Lord and Our Lady loved it still, to the end, partly because of the memory of St Joseph, partly in the way which we love the place in which we spend our early years; no matter how it treats us afterwards, that love stays on. Thus, unlike Capharnaum or Corozain, Nazareth was not destroyed; Nazareth did not understand, just because it was the Prophet's own city; for this very reason it was excused, a wonderful lesson to us of the way in which God forgives those he loves... the peace lives on, or did a few years ago, the peace of the family; carpenters still ply their trade by the wayside, their shops open to the

---

[33] *Hey, You!*, (Burns & Oates 1955), p83

street; here humble folk stand to gossip, while grubby infants sprawl upon the ground's carpets of shaving and sawdust.

But what is all this about, you will say? What have I come to see? And with a shout of joy I can say, 'Nothing more, just this...' That is the supreme delight, that is where you learn to understand the Gospel, not in this particular building, not in this relic of Our Lady's veil. Here on the hilltop, so often spoken of by Our Lord, you feel the good tidings of the Gospel, just as later in Jerusalem or by the Dead Sea, you can breathe the evil blowing in your nostrils. Here the colossal fact is that the memory leaps at sudden glimpses; a maid carrying water in a pot on her head, a sparrow twittering in the cypress tree, children sitting in the market-place, who crying to their companions say, 'We have piped to you and you have not danced.' Here you get all this, because Jesus loved the small things of the world, which are really the big things, if we can only see it that way...

So, through the hills of Galilee, you feel like singing all the way... till you see there below in blue serenity, the palm clustered shore of Lake Genesareth, the Sea of Galilee. This was the way the way Our Lord came... this, all this, was what Christ left when he went up to Jerusalem. We do not have to minimise the humanity of Christ. Many would overemphasise it; but let us do justice to God made man. He had the heart of a man which felt and loved as a man. You only have to read the parables to see the love for the flowers of the field, for the harvest, for the people round about him... (34)

Michael did not take to Jerusalem as he had Galilee, as he makes clear at the beginning of Chapter 14:

I often felt unhappy at entering Jerusalem. I do not think it was only the fact that I went without a military leave or duty pass. I think it must have had the same sort of atmosphere at the preaching of the gospel, but then atmospheres are very subjective so I may have imagined the whole thing. At any rate I found Galilee simple, open, full of the beauty of nature; so too, indeed, are the surroundings of Jerusalem; but the city itself is close, jealous, shut up in its own thoughts and schemes... it has the bitter hypocritical taint of the Pharisee and Sadducee.

---

34 Ibid, pp84-86

Yet, it is this very atmosphere which bring alive Jesus' Passion so vividly for him that he wants to encourage others to seek the same experience.

If you ever go to Jerusalem, try to go in Holy Week; the experience must live with you as long as you breathe… What is there to draw the mind and heart to Jerusalem? It is just that possibility for the ordinary person of making the Gospel live. Until we are capable of the higher unions of prayer, we need some of St Ignatius' 'composition of place'… the whole of liturgy is made not to be a dead thing, cut off from the people, unintelligible. It is meant to live, to sweep up the laity as well as the clergy in its beauty and mystery and significance… That is why in Jerusalem, you have such a wonderful chance to take your place beside Christ in his Passion during Holy Week. For the basis of Catholicism is to live in Christ while Christ lives in you; it is more than that, it is to spread that life of Christ to those around you, but that, too, you can only do, when you are filled with Christ yourself. See then how the Passion lives again in Jerusalem.

Holy Week 1946 certainly seems to have filled Michael with Christ – and to have changed his life. His description of it begins with Palm Sunday. 'The beginning of the Passion is triumph, the way Judas thought it should be worked, the way so obviously wrong to the Son of God, the way we have to learn all our lives to avoid, that is the way of praise and power and earthly success. Each Palm Sunday, then, the people gather on the brow of the hill called Olivet, and carrying palms and olives, great branches of them', wind their way down into the valley, past the spot where Jesus wept over Jerusalem. 'There it lies in all its magnificence, the noble buildings of the temple dominating the foreground'. The procession then moves on down to the brook Kedron, and the Vale of Josaphat, and climbs up again, everybody 'waving their greenery shouting in triumph, singing Hosannas, as they enter the gates of the city. The sun beats down, the olive trees shimmer silvery in the hot breeze, the people rejoice that Jerusalem has recognised its King.'

After the strong emotions of Palm Sunday, there is a need to reflect and pause, and time to do so:

...There was still that day or two to pass before Christ was to die, and during those days, he taught in the temple, and walked each evening back over Olivet to Bethany, to the house of Simon, to Martha and Mary. Here on his way, he saw and cursed the fig tree, so that it withered away and so today you can imagine the feeling of Christ as you climb the rough paths under the hot spring sun; and you can see how he turned to account each passing event to teach a lesson to his disciples... the lessons they had to learn, if they were to bear fruit.

But soon it is Holy Thursday – and Michael's leave is coming to an end:

Thursday quickly follows Sunday, especially when it is the last week of the holidays as it were... nowadays the commemoration of the Passion ... begins near the scene of the Last Supper on Mount Sion, outside the present walls of the city. Here the Franciscans hold a service; and immediately after a hymn being sung they all leave the chapel, and wind along the rugged path, down into the deep valley, and then climbing slightly, across the brook, reach the cool dappled darkness of Gethsemane. In recent years, a basilica has been built in the garden, a regular memorial to a unity of nations which nothing else can forge... and for one hour they watch with Christ, and do not many eyes grow heavy in that hour? Mine certainly did... There, was however, no rest for Our Lord that night.

Michael goes on to describe a visit to the church built on the supposed site of the House of Caiaphas – and then how 'the very truth of the whole Gospel story is borne in your minds as you trudge coldly back into the city, for from the depth of the night, a cock crows.' Is it fanciful to view this incident as having spoken particularly to him in Holy Week 1946? Certainly, it seems implicit in the way he continues:

we are apt to think of this little incident as untoward. Not so at all; it was an everyday occurrence, even in the city; and for this very reason Jesus Christ used it, as he did other common objects, to teach Peter, and not only Peter but every future man, to feel his own individual denial of Christ whenever a cock crows.

So the night passes

and brings the awful emptiness of Good Friday... Of the Way of the
Cross what shall I say?... the first Way of the Cross was the public way,
the street. And what a street; again, it is not the same today, but it is not
likely to have been much better or much different in the days of Simon
the Cyrenean. The rough, uneven cobbles are often jagged-edged, often
slippery; the distance is not great, but much is uphill; a quarter of a mile
– that is about all; yet it takes some twenty minutes to negotiate at a slow
pace. For the way passes through the bazaar; here on the eve of the
Pasch, all Jerusalem, and much of the rest of Palestine is pushing, hag-
gling, whining; the streets themselves are narrow; on each side is a ser-
ried mass of shops encroaching their booths on the already overcrowd-
ed way; there are shops of cobblers, of trinket-makers, stalls of unleav-
ened bread, piles of vegetables, oranges and herbs, the slim carcasses of
Paschal lambs; here a greasy man lazily stirs a sizzling pan of spiced
meats, the air is filled with garlic...

...I used often to wonder how it was that Our Lady could speak to Jesus,
and Veronica wipe his face even, as he went along, surrounded by
guards. Now I can understand; in the thronging thoroughfare, if you are
flattened against the house walls or shop fronts, you could still put out
your hand and touch the person passing in the centre of the street. So
too, he falls, falls upon the cobbles, all slippery with water, dung or
blood from slaughtered animals...

For Michael, there is a sharp contrast between the chaos of the Way – and
the starkness of Calvary itself.

Of Calvary, I can say nothing; whether it is the rush and scurry of several different services, or the quiet peace of night time, there is a wonder
about Calvary... On Good Friday, it is the loneliest place in the world,
because the world has deserted God, and so deserted itself, and plunged
into nonsensical isolation. The real awfulness of what man can do weighs
down upon you on Calvary, until it is almost unbearable... (35)

In 1997, just after Michael died, there was published the last of his three
volumes of *Reflections through the Church's Year*, his offering for *Year C*.

---

35 Ibid, pp91-97

In his meditation for Palm Sunday, he offered a fuller and more directly personal account of his experience that Good Friday over fifty years earlier.

> Good Friday for me in 1946 was very different from any other. I was in Jerusalem as a serving army officer, doing peacekeeping duties but I had got leave during Holy Week... On Friday, I followed the Way of the Cross from the palace of Pilate – *Ecce Homo* [Behold the man] along the streets to reach the Church of the Holy Sepulchre...

> ...I found a corner high up in the Holy Sepulchre basilica and I was able to sit, out of the way and practically unseen. Hour after hour went past. Many came to look round, to kneel, to pray. But this was not disturbing, rather it was like the tide of life ebbing and flowing, while I was blessed by being at a still centre. I cannot say anything too specific. There was no thunder or lightning, no voice, no bolt from the blue. But I was there and I sank more and more deeply in the desolation of Calvary. Christ cried out 'My God! My God! Why have you forsaken me?' Christ breathed 'I thirst' – 'into your hands' – 'it is finished' – Christ died and Mary had her heart pierced as the lance pierced her son, and received his dead body in her arms. Then the tomb was closed. They went sadly, unbelievingly, hopelessly away as the Sabbath evening began. For me, too, the tomb was closed; they shut the Church of the Holy Sepulchre and I went back to my hostel room – empty, desolate, ravaged, but also with foreknowledge of the Resurrection. (36)

Early on Sunday morning he returns – but to a very different atmosphere, as he describes in *Hey, You!*:

> Calvary is incomplete without the Sepulchre. Failure is incomplete without triumph as its outcome. The Gospel would have been vain if there had been no Resurrection, and so, without a doubt, my selfish joy was full at that pale time before the dawn, the time of the holy women. All the streets are sleeping, except for the twitter of birds, and a few beggars crouched in the doorways. The Church of the Holy Sepulchre is dark, but lights glimmer from Calvary and from the Tomb; near the entrance to the tomb itself sits young brother Francis; his face is not unlike that of his holy

---

36 *Reflections through the Church's Year – Year C*, (McCrimmons, 1997), pp51-52

father, the poor man of Assisi... but now brother Francis rests his dark shorn head upon his roughened hands, wearily... Holy Week has taxed him to the limit, young though he is; for since Wednesday he has only snatched three hours' sleep; yet he rises to make room so that we too can kneel and catch the first glimpse of Easter as the newly consecrated host is raised by the priest over the stone slab of the sepulchre – *Resurrexit sicut dixit, alleluia.* [He has risen as he said, alleluia.]

The week had not finished: Michael still had an Easter Monday trip to Emmaus, and

> one more lesson to learn, a lesson we could each well take to heart... the lesson of breaking of bread in which the two disciples knew Our Lord, in which we know Our Lord, in which for the rest of time, Our Lord unites his Mystical Body – the Church...

The road to Emmaus

> is not a road; the country road of Ireland is better than this bullock track. From the last scattered houses of Jerusalem, you plunge straight-away into the rocky countryside, where much of the corn falls on bad ground, though the rest is already 'white for the harvest' at this time of year. Set high above the great coastal plain, the hills fall right away from Emmaus, leaving it perched in space; while sweeping down to the blue floor of the distant Mediterranean, all the land lies rich and green, dappled with splashes of poppy and the flare of the yellow mustard. The air is clear with the newness of the new dawn, with the clarity of the Resurrection. All is beauty, peace, the silence of the country, which is always full of minute sounds. The tranquillity of the Risen Christ has touched Emmaus... it is summed up in the Mass, said among the foundations believed to be those of the house of Cleophas. The rising sun slants through the air, where the birds already echo the alleluias of the liturgy. And this liturgy is made to live again, not only in the literal breaking of bread in the sacrifice, but also in the ancient custom long established, by which the friars set forth a repast of wine or coffee and fresh rolls for all comers on this day, that they too may feel the fellowship of the Church in the breaking of bread. (37)

---

[37] *Hey, You!*, pp97-98

What happened when Michael returned from Jerusalem to his Battalion? Was it at this time that he returned to the sacraments? In *Go in Peace*, he described his own experience of confession, and wrote how after he 'fell away from both belief and practice', his 'subsequent return was not easy' – 'After God had resurrected my belief, I had to face confession after a long and by no means sinless period of army life.' [38]

Perhaps that happened a little earlier – because it must have been soon after this Holy Week that Michael approached the Chaplain of his Battalion and told him he wanted to be a priest. The stress on the liturgy and the eucharist in those two chapters quoted at length from *Hey, You!* seem to have been the consequence of his experiences in the nine years between that Holy Week and the book's publication in 1955. In 1946 it is quite possible that the fellowship experienced with the friars on Mount Tabor and at Emmaus had as much influence – certainly Michael's primary motivation in putting himself forward was firmly people-oriented. As he described in *Living Priesthood*, 'one way and another God found me out again largely in the disillusion of the after-war period. It was then I thought of priesthood. Realising I had been reclaimed by God or more correctly – I had come to his welcome and love, I wanted to help other people.'

When Michael told him of his desire to be a priest, the Chaplain asked him why he wanted to try to become one. 'I said to help people. He asked if I did not see Mass as being the centre of what a priest is. I simply said I did not, I wanted to help people' [39], causing the Chaplain to take a step backwards.

Nor did Michael conform in other ways. His wartime experiences, and the desire they gave him to work for his men and their families, prompted him to apply not for a religious order – at that time the normal refuge of upper-middle-class English Catholics with a religious vocation – but for the diocesan priesthood.

---

38 *Go in Peace*, p15
39 *Living Priesthood*, p19

In *Living Priesthood*, Michael described what happened next. 'Just as I somehow got into Oxford and Sandhurst by the back door, so with Seminary training. Cardinal Griffin when he interviewed me' – in August 1946 – 'thought I was thirty-four when in reality I was twenty-four. He had already made arrangements to send me to the Beda College in Rome for late vocations. His face fell when I declared my true age, but to the Beda I went, paid for as further education by a grateful government.' (40) A later article – for the *Beda Review* of 1985 – offered one or two additional details: 'An old Beda man, Mgr Vernon Johnson, had been responsible for getting my name to Westminster, while I was still soldiering in Palestine. He it was who told me that I was to go to the Beda and talked of "late vocations". But when I arrived at Archbishop's House, still in the uniform of a major of the Brigade of Guards, I found that while the Archbishop knew about my rank etc., he had the idea I was thirty-four when I was only twenty-four. He seemed taken aback, but the arrangements had already been made.' (41)

Thus it was that in October 1946, two months short of his 25th birthday, Michael began life as a seminarian in Rome.

---

40 Ibid, pp19-20
41 'Musings on Late Vocations', p58 in the *Beda Review* (Rome, 1985)

CHAPTER TWO

The Beda – the first two years

JOCK DALRYMPLE

In 1953, three years after he left the college, Michael wrote an enthusiastic article for the *Beda Review* entitled 'The Beda As I Knew It.' In it he confessed that 'like the majority of ordinary Catholics in England' he had never heard of the Beda until he was told this was the place where he would study for the priesthood. He also described the challenges that had faced him in the weeks before he went there – both the 'petty difficulties which rise up at the thought of vocation' which 'loom very large when the devil, world and flesh combine with many of one's friends to ridicule the idea of entering a seminary' – and his fears as to the exact nature of life in such an institution:

> How could I get down to books, to philosophy; how study between walls? When people asked me about theology, I knew nothing... I could serve Mass, but singing and ceremonies! What was (or were?) metaphysics, and did a priest know all about something called Epistemology? Should I walk again in a crocodile after drilling a Battalion? Was it true there were regulations about smoking, one bath a week, and compulsory football on half-holidays? [1]

During the Second World War the Beda had been evacuated to Upholland in Lancashire. In October 1946, the month Michael arrived in Rome, it reopened in its old home, No.67, Via di S. Nicolo da Tolentino, near the Piazza Barberini. The Beda had originally been founded – in 1852 – for convert clergy, but after the Second World War some late vocations had been 'filtered in to widen the "feel" of the college.' In consequence, Michael 'found a number of ex-servicemen alongside me, together with

---

1 'The Beda As I Knew It', in the *Beda Review* (March 1953), p46

some very senior men, many of whom had been clergy, and even canons in the Church of England. I should think the average age was about fifty, with myself very much at the lower end of the range, and one or two over seventy.' (2)

From the perspective of 1953, Michael looked back with affection, indeed almost with nostalgia on his four years there. His worst fears had not been realised, because the Beda, under the wise stewardship of Mgr Charles Duchemin, its rector since 1928, had recognised that 'the independent fully developed man must be brought under discipline with wise handling.' In addition, writing as Michael was from his third floor room in his first parish of St Patrick's, Soho, he was all too aware of how liberal for the time his formation had been. In his opinion, the Beda's ten rules – 'not too little and not too much' – had provided a good 'framework for mental and spiritual growth' which could be 'carried on into the parish, rather than being discarded with a sigh of relief.' (3)

However, twenty-four years later, in the brief three pages in *Living Priesthood* that describe this period in his life, Michael writes in a rather less positive tone.

> It was hard, physically, mentally, socially and spiritually. After being a Company Commander in a Guards Regiment with respect, power, authority and responsibility I found it very hard to be nobody, with nothing. In a way, I did not know what I was doing; the philosophy books in Latin made me no clearer and nor did the lectures. The spiritual director was dry as dust though learned and holy. The college life was interesting, but we were both cold and hungry in the first post-war years. Rather lost, feeling unguided and alone, I took to stringent living. My motive for joining had been to help others. Apart from those among whom I lived, there was no one to help. (4)

Two approaches learnt during the war sustained him. The first had been picked up

---

2 'Musings on Late Vocations', in the *Beda Review* (Rome 1985), p58
3 'The Beda As I Knew It', p48
4 *Living Priesthood* (McCrimmons, 1994), p20

47

in the East End of London as bombs fell and again especially in Italy. Psychologically, I discovered that in fear when all I wanted to do was run away, it helped to do everything exaggeratedly slowly; not only did this instil calm in myself, it encouraged reassurance in others. Secondly, I learnt that if you have cowardly instincts, as I do, the only hope is to face the fear, the unknown, the threat. My spiritual help at this time was the passage in Luke about Jesus in Gethsemane. I was not learned in scriptural analysis; the translation I knew told me of Jesus: 'being in agony, he prayed the longer.' (Luke 22: 44). The Jerusalem Bible tells me 'In his anguish he prayed more earnestly.' At the time, that translation would not have been so effective as the one I had. I felt Jesus had gone out into the desert in his earlier days to face the evil one and himself in aloneness; later in the garden, he had prayed the longer: this was language I understood. (5)

In consequence, prayer and penance became the central foundations of Michael's life.

To some extent I had been taught what discipline meant in the army. They had said that no one gets anywhere without hard slog and self-discipline. I had learnt then the hard way. Now I had found it to be true. It now tied up with Christ and his life. So I set myself a routine of observing the *magnum silentium*, the silence following night prayers, when we were supposed to go to our rooms and not talk to each other. There was a lot of temptation to go off to coffee parties; not going, I came to feel isolated. I made a bedtime for myself, introducing sleeping on the floor and getting up to pray in the middle of the night. I rose early before the bell to get additional time for prayer. I also took to slipping away in the afternoon when many had a siesta or went walking. I located two churches which had exposition, one of which, S. Claudio in Piazza San Silvestro near the English church, kept open all during the afternoon. There I often literally sweated it out, in dull, dumb, boring knee-aching slog. I slept there often; I seldom had much sense of prayer. Yet I went back there again and again, day by day, like a drowning man grabbing at a lifeline… I have often said since then that it was there and in the chapel of the Beda that I learnt anything I did learn. (6)

---

5 Ibid, pp20-21
6 Ibid, p21

In *Day by Day* Michael offered an alternative perspective on the way his prayer developed during these early years after the rediscovery of his faith and his going to the seminary. Initially, it was

> contact with the desire to work for the men and their families with whom I was associated at the end of World War II which drove me to God and prayer... But having realised the need I had through human need, I came quickly to find the emphasis in my case swinging onto the 'God dimension' as in fact of prior importance. (7)

He likened the process, once it had begun, to aspects of drug addiction and alcoholism:

> The desire to pray can often be a sense of being repelled rather than attracted, only the 'hangover' is pre-prayer, whereas with the other two addictions it is post. The almost nausea can carry on into the prayer time, and even beyond, but despite that the draw to come back for more is insidious. What is more as with alcohol, the frequency and quality grow. But of course it would be better to liken the process to the development of a relationship of love, which is in truth what it is. As the lover cannot bear to part from the beloved, so the one who 'gets hooked on God' wants to be, consciously or unconsciously, always close to the One, deeply, silently, intently, lovingly, whether in prayer absolute or a prayer-work-service-love relationship.

> At least this is what happened to me. It was at first an urgent seeking inquest of belief, then glimmering, then blinding, then dully, dryly, dreary... In the beginning, I did an awful lot of work myself, and felt the time given, the tiredness, the battle with sleep, the distractions all worthwhile – formative, ascetic, fruitful. Regularity begun at this point soon grew into familiarity or routine; but this in turn gave way to a rhythm like breathing, which is essential, yet not often realised in day to day living. (8)

At the same time Michael also acknowledged the positive effect on him of living with his fellow students, most of whom were older than him. At first he had been sceptical about them, especially the 'converts'. 'Like so

---

7 *Day by Day* (Mayhew-McCrimmon, 1972), p14
8 Ibid, p12-13

many Catholics, I had had little contact with other denominations on a religious level; what I had had been of the back-slapping type.' Indeed as one who 'almost despised parsons', his initial attitude to them was 'silly old codgers, they'll never make Catholic priests'. Soon however – 'a humbling thought, a shaming thing' – he began to realise how remarkable many of them were and indeed how 'God... loved them beyond beloved me' – and 'liking and admiration filtered in, until there grew a determination to assist in some small way the efforts of these men to reach the priesthood, rejoicing in the new life opened up to them.' (9)

Elsewhere he wrote how any humility he possessed had been learnt from the 'men of stature' he met in the Beda who had

> come in all simplicity for God's service late in life, often having served so long and well already, submitting to discipline and becoming as little children; I learned it from those who had belonged to other Christian churches, had found their way from quite eminent positions and now rubbed shoulders with me who was a mere babe in religion, and yet took me as an equal and opened the door of friendship. (10)

In addition, it was through some of these men that Michael realised in a new way 'the value of a friend older than myself who could be really close and really a friend, so that he could tell me off, teach me by example and lead me by his matured personality and wisdom, which was often so distilled by years, humility and suffering as to be as simple as a dove.' In this regard, he singled out "Pop' Oakes ordained about sixty-eight and Colonel Schomberg at about seventy-two' who 'both taught me much.' (11)

In 'The Beda As I Knew It', while reflecting on the value of his prolonged contact with these 'ordinary converts', Michael commented on his own conversion – and the way that his experience of life affected the process of his formation in seminary.

---

9 'The Beda As I Knew It', p47
10 *Living Priesthood*, p21
11 'The Beda As I Knew It', p58

In a sense, too, the Catholic I represent has had his own experience of conversion – conversion from being a layman to the idea of being a priest. The longer he lives in the world, in many ways, the bigger the gap between himself and the priesthood. But he knows better than a young student some pitfalls of the presbytery. He knows what it is to pluck up the courage to ring the bell for confession, to be told there are no confessions. He has met the sincere, but nevertheless hostile housekeeper, who regards any attempt to see the priest as intrusion upon his and her own privacy. He has met the priest who will not tolerate a layman's help as though fearing for his own prerogative. He has seen immense goodness and the sadness of mediocrity. He has felt the power of the holy priest and come to realise the intense need for spirituality in the material world – a need learnt from life, not from a lecture. And so it is that he comes almost as a reformer, himself to be re-formed. (12)

His experience, therefore, influenced the way he learnt – and in this particular article Michael was rather more positive than he would be in *Living Priesthood* about the value of his studies:

through the mill of philosophy and theology, his experience becomes framed in the structure of theory. Muddled feelings, thoughts, ideas are crystallised. His education in the worldly sense may be vast, but here he seeks and finds a codification. Hence the lectures are more those of a university than a schoolroom. His own philosophy must grow now upon the bare bones of Thomism given by the professor: his practical and prayerful knowledge of theology learnt from Mass and Catechism deepens in the beauty of the dogmatic approach to the Eucharist and Trinity. But the plunge from an active life, into *per se* and *per accidens* is none the less arduous... (13)

Quite apart from the travails of study, during these years Michael also faced times of crisis – 'In the middle because of trying to cope with what was meant by celibacy and how it fitted with sexuality and intimacy and friendship, I nearly packed up before I broke down' – and of being drawn in very different directions; on the one hand he felt attracted by the con-

---

12 'The Beda As I Knew It', p47
13 Ibid

templative life – 'every now and then throughout the four years, I leaned towards the monastery, silence, the life devoted totally to God in prayer' – while at other times,

> I wanted to run away altogether because of insecurity, doubts as to the church, the priesthood and God himself. Several times offers were made of lucrative jobs in the world, and there were two or three marriageable young women both in Rome and in England, whom I had known when I was more glamorously clad as a Guards officer... When the invitations to dinner came in, and were allowed by the Rector, accepted and enjoyed, the floor afterwards seemed rather harder and the night vigil very much alone. (14)

As a way of coping with these night vigils and the other challenges of seminary life, Michael sought 'ways and means of toughening' himself. Crucially, this included searching for 'types' of self-giving in Rome and further afield. In March 1947 he discovered 'a shining and thrilling example', Padre Pio (1887-1968). (15)

In an appendix to *Living Priesthood*, Michael reflected at length on how this first meeting with Padre Pio changed his life.

> I hope you have experienced in your life some meeting or awakening of the kind which is the basis for this recollection. If you have not then I hope that God will in his own time give you such a happening, a death and resurrection, because after it life can never be quite the same again. Never quite the same... much fuller and deeper.

> My personal experience was encountering Padre Pio... I suppose I would not be isolated from the feeling of a good number of people when I was first asked to go down Italy from Rome to meet 'the Franciscan friar who has the stigmata, Padre Pio.' Part of me said; 'Good heavens that's the man it was suggested I should go and see when I was a soldier in Italy in World War II and had completely lost all belief. I pooh-poohed the idea then and I'm not going to be involved in that sort of thing now.' Part of me said 'Michael, since then you have come to belief

---

14 *Living Priesthood*, p22
15 Ibid

in God again. What is your faith? Do you put limits to what God can do, if he wants?'

...Frankly, I was queasy at the thought of going, because, despite openness in confession, I was still scared somehow that Padre Pio might (almost magically) see evil in me which would preclude my continuing towards the priesthood.

Padre Pio had been sent to a convent of the Friars Minor Capuchin at San Giovanni Rotondo, Foggia. This is in the mountainous district which forms the 'spur' on the heeled foot of Italy's Adriatic coastline. So we journeyed there to arrive in darkness and chill on a March evening in 1947. That night was spent coldly miserable, shivering in a bed with only one blanket, grateful to be woken at 4.30 in the morning to go to Padre Pio's Mass. But all this added to the sense of repulsion and refusal in my body, mind and heart. ...we went icily through wind and darkness to the convent door, where already at five o'clock people of all sorts were collecting, pressed against the doors, pushing, shoving, even hitting each other... we found ourselves moved towards the rear of the altar, to the sacristy ...we stood and shivered, silently; the small door into the cloister opened, people breathed; 'Padre Padre', and he was there...

Yes, he was there, and at once there were two reactions... Firstly, intense disillusion; a little man, shuffling, irritable with whoever pressed round too close, a 'no-one'. And secondly, a relaxation, a peace and a joy; here was a real person with whom I could be myself, as he was himself. What a relief! No need to pose... just to be me.

I had spoken no word to him. This was just what he felt like.

The Mass followed. It was long (one hour and a half). It was slow. For part of it there was an irritation; for part of it, physical pain in kneeling upright. But gradually a sense of rightness, commitment to sacrifice and passion, a suffering borne with a serenity and peace which I had never experienced, an acceptance of oneness and sharing both with Christ and humanity which was beyond any limit I had reached.

It was not that there was anything startling or exotic. There was no flowing blood from the wounds, or cries or sighs. I was very much relieved.

For me it was a long-drawn-out penitential exercise, when Padre Pio was caught and held in prayer for five or ten minutes at a time, with a concentration which I was normally far from sharing.

Padre Pio drew to the Mass two or three hundred people at 5 am, winter and summer. He had people queuing for his counsel and for sacramental absolution, so that it might take three or four days before your numbered ticket came up. When I knelt before him to lay myself open to God, the beauty and relief was that he was very simple, very ordinary and very reassuring. I went out from the sacristy 'open' confessional knowing more truly why penance is spoken of as 'an encounter with Christ'. It was from this time that I 'found' and used the Jesus prayer with meaning; because of this experience, I understood the word of Jesus: 'More blessed he who has not seen, and has believed...' but I was happy to have 'seen'.

...If anyone was to ask me what was perhaps the most striking characteristic of Padre Pio – from the viewpoint of example to the ordinary people of God – I would without hesitation sum it up in the one word; obedience.

...It is not surprising, if we accept that ultimately all obedience is summed up in the words of Christ about his mother; 'Blessed are they who hear the word of God and keep it.' This Padre Pio did, with love, for the will of God is love...

Michael concluded;

This I know. Once you or I have lived a little in the circle of such a man as Padre Pio, life cannot ever be quite the same again, however much we remain selfish and sinful, forgetful and stupid. That is why in the work of Christ in his world, we need more and more Padre Pios, more Mother Teresas, more Taizés and Ionas. Padre Pio would not have been happy that you simply listened and looked, or read this. He would say to you as he said to me: 'I will always remember you in my prayers – go away now and seek the Lord's will – and do it.' (16)

---

16 Ibid, pp257-262

In five subsequent visits, Michael was to get so close to Padre Pio that the latter used to call him *'Michelino mio'* – 'my little Michael'. In *Hey, You!* – written while Padre Pio was still alive – he summed up the friar's influence on him:

> ...converts are often over-enthusiastic in the eyes of their more staid companions in the faith, and I was, as it were, converted to belief in Padre Pio. This came about by visiting him, because he crystallises what I have been taught, what I had been trying and still am trying to learn of the spiritual life. He emphasises continually and above all other considerations the primary importance of holiness especially in a priest. To this end he focuses everything into love, shown by a complete emptying of self in the service of love, through absolute humility and obedience. This he expresses in the Sacrifice of the Mass, carried on throughout the day in total surrender to God's children. (17)

Later that same year, Michael was introduced to another of the formative and lasting influences on his life, and another 'type' of self-giving, St Thérèse of Lisieux (1873-1897). In the introduction to his short biography of her (1981), he recalled how in the summer of 1947 he had been asked by Mgr Vernon Johnson – who had been responsible for his going to the Beda – to come with him and another friend to spend time in Lisieux. Johnson had been converted to the Roman Catholic Church in the 1920's 'because someone had suggested he should read the autobiography of a young woman, Marie Françoise Thérèse Martin, who had died as a nun in the Carmelite monastery of Lisieux at the early age of twenty-four'. On being 'captured by the spiritual doctrine of the saint', Johnson had gone immediately to Lisieux and been introduced to her sisters who were still members of the community there. He got to know them well and returned frequently, taking Michael with him in 1947 to meet two of the sisters, Pauline and Céline. Michael wrote later, 'it was through him and his close understanding of both the saint and the recollections of her sisters that I was introduced to the background of her life and the simplicity of her unique contribution to spirituality – the Little Way of Spiritual Childhood.'

---

17 *Hey, You!* (Burns & Oates, 1955), p121

Michael

was privileged to visit Alençon where the family originally lived and where Thérèse was born, to spend long hours in the Carmelite chapel, to wander through the house and garden of Les Buissonets, and to stand in the typical French cemetery above Lisieux where Thérèse was originally buried. And all this in the company of Vernon Johnson, who had both come so close to the surviving members of the family and also been so deeply involved with Thérèse's Little Way. (18)

We have two other revealing and contrasting glimpses of Michael in these early years in the seminary. The first is through an article he wrote for the 1948 *Beda Review*, entitled 'An Act of Faith – at the piazza San Pietro in 1947'. In it he described the Easter Sunday Mass of that year celebrated by Pope Pius 12th, and the blessing *Urbi et Orbe* [for the city and the world] that always follows it, revealing himself as already possessing a fresh and readable writing style, and as unexpectedly ultramontane in his youthful fervour. In the light of recent negative publicity surrounding that Pope's wartime stance, the article also provides an interesting example of the immense admiration felt for Pius by many people – including Michael – in the early post war years.

The article begins with a description of the build-up to the Mass:

For days beforehand, those street walls of Rome, which Mussolini had kept unsullied by bills or posters, were plastered with this message, with this cry to the people, with this call for an act of faith...

'During the war, who was it that never deserted Rome? The Duce? The Government? No it was *Il Papa*. Who fed the hungry, clothed the naked, gave refuge to the fugitives? *Il S. Padre*. [The Holy Father] Who came out to pray among the ruins of S. Lorenzo for the safety of the city, for the victims, for their relatives? *Sua Santita*. [His Holiness]'

And now what was the attitude of the people? What was all this anti-clericalism? Why were the corsos and piazzas of Rome full of papers and posters vilifying Christ and His Servant of Servants?

Come then, you people of Rome! *Tutti a S. Pietro a testimoniare la nostra Fede*. [Everybody to St Peter's to witness to our Faith].

---

18 *Thérèse of Lisieux* (Collins, 1981), pp7-8

The sun shone clearly from the deep blue of the sky. It was warm hurrying along through the glinting yellow leaves which still hung above the Tiber. There were many others hurrying too, priests in their long grecas and beaver hats, nuns of every order you have ever known, (and many more you will never know), the rich in heavy coats, the men so truly Roman with their fur collars, the poor with rags, with clogs, with their rosaries... yes they were all hurrying along... to S.Pietro... and so were we.

Michael notes how 'in the Italian crowds, you need a mastery of three things, the smile, the elbow, and the word permesso' and how 'if you are lucky enough to be six feet tall in Italy, you have a perfectly clear field of view in most gatherings,' before displaying an early and characteristic appreciation of the value of using the best available technology – 'Seldom have I heard such effective broadcasting; never before have I heard a better open-air relay of the Holy Sacrifice'. He then continues, rather breathlessly, by describing the logistical challenge presented by due reverence for the consecration.

> *Tutti in Ginocchio!* [Everybody on their knees]. In that tightly wedged piazza, we were all to kneel to adore. How could it be done? It is hard to say; in fact, many never reached their knees, some were almost suspended between one thing and the other, some got to the ground, to feel a great doubt as to whether they would ever stand again.

However,

> as the bell tinkled through the sun-drenched air, there was a deep hush over the multitude, the murmur of the organ only emphasising the true depth of their faith, that greatest of God's gifts, that hardest of tasks, which is for the rich or the poor, the old or the young. 'He gave them power to be made the sons of God, to them that believe in His name'... *DOMINUS ET DEUS MEUS* [My Lord and my God]... The youth ahead with the thick, black, Italian hair, the peasant woman clutching her rosary by my side, her lips moving silently, the ragged, unshaven beggar beyond her, the nuns, the child held by her father to see the Elevation...

57

Communion follows, the Mass ends and the crowd is 'still quiet, still attentive, still reverent.' It has been 'a memorable act of faith, a counter-blow at the forces of anti-religion, an object lesson for the future'. And now everybody waits on for the Pope's Easter blessing:

> ...as the glass doors sweep open, a wave of feeling, intense, sponta-neous, fills each watching one below, until in a second the piazza is a place gone mad, a raging pool of hands and arms, banners and hats, handkerchiefs, anything and everything to add to the tumultuous cry, – *Viva il Papa...* and calmly, slowly, a tiny figure, he appears, embracing us all below with the breadth of his gestures, holding the concentration of a frenzied crowd without speaking a single word. For whole minutes he stands there... Now, at last he raises hands in command, and in the silence that follows he addresses us... I must say as strongly as I can how impressive was the part when he referred to the presence of anti-Christian activities in a growing scale in Rome, Italy and the world. When he said that each had to be for Christ, with a spontaneous cry, '*per Christo*' the crowd answered him... Indeed *Il Papa* has the heart of the people of Rome. It is said that next to God he is looked upon as the sav-iour of Rome... Once more he appears, once more he blesses... and he is gone... [19]

The second glimpse of Michael in these years comes in a story he later recounted in *Day by Day* – a tale strangely complementary to 'An Act of Faith' in the way it brings alive both the Rome of the late 1940's, with all its accompanying political tensions, and Michael's own personal struggles:

> It was a very hot sultry sirocco day and in the morning we had a lec-ture on the sacrament of penance; it was very hot in the lecture room, the sun beating down on the tin roof, and I was in a terribly bolshy mood about the whole thing and very sleepy. The lecturer started off by say-ing; 'In the twentieth chapter of Saint John, you find the statement of Christ which is the basis for the sacrament of penance, "whose sins you forgive they are forgiven"'. I thought, 'Right. I know that.', and I went to sleep. When I woke up he was saying; 'John 20, whose sins you for-give, they are forgiven.' So I went to sleep again. I woke up and heard

---

19 'An Act of Faith', in *The Beda Book* (London, 1957), pp137-141

'if you want to prove... John 20'. I was absolutely tearing my hair and fed up with the whole thing.

In the afternoon, I had to go on a long, hot walk to see somebody in hospital at the other end of Rome, and there I was in my flat hat and long skirt-like soutane and not able to afford to go by bus because I was a poor student. I was thoroughly fed up, wondering if I had a vocation, whether God existed, why it was so hot, how sweaty I was, the whole thing was absolute hell. I came past the church of Saint John Lateran, and there was no one about; for every one was sensibly having a siesta. Then I came into the little cobbled street near Saint John Lateran and there was a young man sweeping the road, which was a very odd thing to be doing at that time of the day.

As I came past he leaned on his broom and said in his best Italian, could he speak to me, and I said in my worst Italian that I was not Italian, so he said 'Good'. Then he said could I tell him something because he was living with Communists in his lodgings and they were arguing about Scripture and they said to him that there was no place in Scripture where it said anything about the sacrament of penance and could I tell him if this was so! Now I was carrying a little New Testament with me so I brought it out to show him it was in the twentieth chapter of St John and he, of course, was absolutely delighted. [20]

Confession itself had initially presented Michael with a problem when he arrived at the Beda. At the time there was a system by which a priest came in each week to hear confessions and to give a spiritual talk to the students. In *Go in Peace*, Michael recalled how 'most students seemed to go to confession to him. He was very gentle and kind but dry as dust in his spiritual talk to the college. In the confessional he did no more than give a penance and pronounce the words of absolution.' However, soon after that,

I was given an introduction to an elderly priest whom I took to visiting regularly each week. I always went to his room; he was a mine of interest and information, especially on prayer and parish life. Gradually I took to making a periodic confession to him, asking him at the same

---

time for counsel and guidance. I still continued, in between these occasions, to go to the college spiritual director for absolution. [21]

Elsewhere, Michael revealed some more about his guide. 'Very prayerful, very austere, he had tried to refound the male order of Brigittines and failed, so was living out his days as a much loved chaplain to the Little Company of Mary. As I listened to him, over and over again he spoke of: "the daily miracle of a holy life." '[22]

In the two or three years before the elderly priest died, his openness and 'the way in which... he allowed me to get to know him' was 'a new experience.' As a consequence 'I was able in turn to be open with him, so that he also got to know me... It was new to find a priest willing to give me time, to understand my hang-ups and depressions and visions of priesthood while he expounded his ideas on the priestly life. His interest encouraged me in black times, when to me there was a question mark over God's call to serve him through ordination.'

It also opened up for Michael 'the dual possibility in confession of receiving absolution and gaining the benefit of counselling from an older, wiser and holier person.' It was 'one seed which among others widened my mind to different approaches to the sacrament' and 'set me to wondering about the availability of such help to the man and woman in the street, in the life I had lived before coming to the college.' [23] He would spend much of his later life as a priest offering such help.

---

21 *Go in Peace* (McCrimmons, 1990), p15
22 *Living Priesthood*, p13
23 *Go in Peace*, p15-16

CHAPTER THREE

The Beda: 1948–1950

JOCK DALRYMPLE

In September 1948, Michael's first cousin, Jock Dalrymple, joined him in Rome, to begin his studies for the diocesan priesthood at the Scots College, three minutes' walk from the Beda. Jock's father, Sir Hew Dalrymple, had

been Michael's main inspiration and support within the family since his mother's death – and indeed became for him 'the embodiment of the devout life' (1) – and Michael set out to provide similar support for Jock who was nearly seven years his junior. Neither had really known the other up to that point but soon a close relationship developed, with Michael becoming Jock's mentor as well as friend. Indeed over the next thirty-seven years until his untimely death in 1985, the latter kept and filed away every letter Michael wrote him. (2)

Michael with his uncle, Hew Dalrymple, and his cousin, Elsie Gibbs. Rome 1954

1 Athirst for God: daily readings with St Francis de Sales, (DLT, 1985), pviii

2 Jock Dalrymple arrived at the Scots College in 1948 as a twenty year old, fresh from two years in the Scots Guards. He was ordained a priest for the archdiocese of St Andrews & Edinburgh in July 1954, and spent the next thirty-one years working in that diocese. He was successively, philosophy tutor at the diocesan seminary of Drygrange, assistant priest at St Mary's Cathedral in Edinburgh, spiritual director (1960-1970) at Drygrange, University Chaplain (1970-74) at St Andrews University, and parish priest (1975-1985) of St Ninian's, Restalrig in Edinburgh. Like Michael, he became well known for his books on prayer and the Christian life, his retreat-giving, his 'open-house' presbytery, and his radical and challenging lifestyle. Sadly, we only have one half of the correspondence between Michael and Jock – none of Jock's letters to Michael seem to have survived.

The letters Michael wrote to Jock in the two years they were together in Rome until the former's ordination in April 1950, and return to England in June, are far and away the best source for Michael's life in these years. In one of them, written on January 1st 1950, discussing the essence of St Thérèse's teachings he states 'I have always been given to understand that if you want to know a person, it is best to read the letters rather than the "works" '. In the light of that, in this chapter these extraordinary documents will be allowed to speak for themselves. Admittedly there are elements that jar to modern eyes and ears – a certain social diffidence and clumsy self-deprecation on a personal level; and, more fundamentally, some theological attitudes which reflect the more life-denying aspects of pre-Vatican II Catholicism, including an un-nuanced stress on the value of suffering apparently for its own sake. But when reading them, it is important to remember that they are the product of a different, harsher and more ascetic age and that, in the decades that followed, Michael's spirituality would develop and grow.

Moreover, these letters do illustrate clearly the remarkable extent to which after a mere two years at the Beda, Michael had already attained a considerable degree of spiritual maturity and wisdom, and had quickly developed into a wise guide of souls. They also offer a vivid picture of the life of a seminarian in Rome just after the war. Above all, so much of what he wrote as a young man of twenty-eight over fifty years ago, reassures, inspires and challenges as forcefully today as it must have done his even younger cousin at the time. Incidentally, the letters were written as they read, their fluency mirrored by the way there is scarcely a crossing out in any of them.

The first letter from Michael kept by Jock was written by him on the Feast of the Epiphany, January 6th, 1949.

> It was lovely seeing you over here last night. Thank you so much for coming – and I hope it was fun for you. I fear I was a very bad host; I always am...
>
> ...I only got your letter yesterday – you see what the posts are like in Rome! It is excellent to think that you are happy at the Scots College – a very excellent thing indeed – but as you know happiness is not every-

The opening two paragraphs in Michael's first letter to Jock, January 6th, 1949

thing and God is generally very good about letting us down lightly. You have been very generous in giving up your life to him and He will always outdo you in generosity. But giving is a continual job and He just wants it all the time, in joy and sorrow. When the time comes and everything is quite black and impossible and there is every reason for not carrying on, that is just the time when God is showing you most love, and by hanging on you are showing most love to Him. But of course one of the main trials is that we cannot see this at the time.

...I always fear, and I expect uncle Hew [Jock's father] has said much the same, that the emphasis is inclined to shift wrongly onto the passing of examinations etc. Really, the only thing that matters is your life of prayer, which must be developed. Unfortunately, the majority of students coming out of seminary can't pray, and never learn in all their lives, partly through negligence, through the general opinion being slightly against intense prayer, and also because they are afraid of what it means. I feel, don't you, that if we are to be priests, please God, we must 'go the whole hog' – hold back nothing.

Well, the only way is by prayer, because if we come closer to God He will give us all we need. You may have come across the philosophical saying *nemo dat quod non habet* [no one gives what he does not have]. That sums it up; unless we have a deep spiritual life based on the love of God, we cannot give it to our parishioners. If we make ourselves more and more perfectly open to receive God's grace, He will pour it into us, and we, as His instruments can pour it upon others. But we cannot pour out what is not inside us – hence the bad sermons we get constantly, which are based on a theological textbook and not the love of God.

I feel all this very strongly, and so I write it to you... I don't want to exclude the amount of hard work which must be put into books. But in my opinion, and it has some backing among the saints, if the study were cut down and the prayer increased, the result would be doubly effective... forgive me, because I know what I say is true, even when contradicted. Better any day to be a holy priest than a learned one.

Pray for me. I have so much to learn and to do. I pray constantly for you to do God's work with ever greater love. You know St Augustine's phrase – 'Love, and do what you will' – or St Thérèse, 'Love is the only thing that really matters.' Forgive me,

Affectionately, Michael.

Michael's next letter is undated and includes a reflection on the uncertain political climate of the late 1940's and what seemed like its possible consequences:

We are, of course, living at a very tremendous time, so far as I can see. And though the emphasis with you will be upon the study while you are in Rome, it is quite obvious when we are faced with doings like the trial of Cardinal Mindszenty[3], that we may all be reduced in a less pub-

---

3 Cardinal Mindszenty, the leader of the Hungarian church, was arrested just after Christmas Day, 1948, as the communist governments of Eastern Europe began to persecute the church. He was tortured in prison and beaten into signing a confession. His trial in early 1949 was the nastiest of several show-trials of bishops. During the 1956 Revolution, he was freed and found refuge in the American embassy, where he remained for fifteen years.

lic way to the same sort of thing; and then the only thing that counts is a burning love of God and a close union with Him to keep us from yielding and denying Him.

We live in security and routine, but the routine ends with the end of the seminary. After that you have to make it yourself. Unless you have become devoted to prayer, it will be squeezed out of your life – and prayer is the only fertiliser which will bring your harvest field to ripen.

On 7th March Michael is writing again; his initial remarks illustrate a characteristic diffidence, but then he moves on to spiritual matters and the subject of St Thérèse, and freshness and confidence shine through once more:

Thank you so much. Your letter gave me a much needed kick in the pants! In the first place, how kind of you to write and thank me for a thing which was far more pleasure to the host than it can ever have been to the guests. I make a habit (selfish, lazy etc.) of never entertaining in my room. Hence, badly laid on, all the product of others, and due to their kindness. It is a real joy to have you over – but please understand I hesitate to ask you all to come. I can only say, if this party was a success, do let it be repeated: it does me good, if you do not suffer.

Ref. the rest of your letter. I can only say – and my poor life is becoming more and more a repetition – *Deo Gratias*. Since I came to know St Thérèse, I have placed the 'grace' of conversion to an understanding of her very high in the lives of men and women today. It must be a sort of grace, because it just comes and the way it can develop is amazing. Always remember that she made a summary on her death bed of what all the good saints were taught – 'Love is the only thing that matters' – how near to St Paul or St Augustine or St John of the Cross or St John or Our Lord himself! It is all the Law and the Prophets!

Don't mind about suffering. You will suffer and the greatest agony will be being unable to suffer gladly. Don't bother too much about little faults: the closer you come to a light (in this case God) the more clearly you see the dirt, fallen hairs, dandruff clinging to your cassock. Well and good. But keep your eyes fixed on the light and not on chasing the hairs, which then simply turn to hares, animated by the Devil.

In other words, you seek the love of God and not perfection – you may say it is the same, but there is a chasm of difference between the two,

65

because the latter can only be a picture made by yourself, and God may will that you never reach what we would envisage as 'perfection'; while you do come very far up the path of love, by offering your imperfection.

I must go to bed. Tomorrow (8th) is the 4th anniversary of Mummy's death – how lovely to feel she is looking down, please God, and cheering us on from the edge of Heaven, with Jean [Jock's sister who died in 1947] and St Thérèse and all the rest. It makes us all so very close in this petty little world of ours, while God only asks us to live by the "sacrament of the present moment" as de Caussade calls it.

... Life gets no easier – but who would wish that it should? We can only join in 'singing the mercies of the Lord' – that He should stoop so low to pick us up so tenderly. He is always good and sweet and so gentle, and so very very patient with His toddlers, like you and I who are always tripping over imaginary bumps on the carpet of life...

PS. Generally (not that there is any very set rule in spiritual things) the time of joy is before the time of trial, and not vice versa, as one often expects in 'human affairs' – the prize for the fight is given one not as a reward but as a pledge, so that when the trial comes, you have every reason for the trust you cannot 'feel'.

The next letter is written on March 19th, the feast of St Joseph, 'patron of contemplative souls'. Jock's mother and brother have been staying, and have conveyed a request from his father that Jock be allowed to come home for the summer, unlike his fellow students at the Scots College who were to remain behind at the College's summer villa.

... It is I who should be thanking the Dalrymples for the real joy of the past ten days. Unfortunately I am a very stupid and unsociable fellow; really, there is no reason for me to appear busy and as for prayers, that as you know must pervade the whole of life, for as Cassian says, 'He prays but little and but badly who only prays when on his knees.' So that is a thing to be developed, by the grace of God as time goes by.

...Rome is overwhelming; perhaps one does not properly enjoy it until one grows into it. At least I feel so, and they may find little things which pop-up suddenly when the rest has become a vague blur in the shades of memory. I am sure it will add to their love of the Church and of God.

...Now, what I write you must always take with a pinch of salt, because I have no authority except my limited experience. Do not worry about the summer. Try so far as possible to put it out of your mind... In all these things, one must be under the will of God, which is what the superiors decide. It is always hard to be an exception – apart from anything else, it makes for unpleasantness among one's fellows – adding to the always delicate problem of class prejudice. But there again it can be turned to profit. Objectively, to stay at the villa is the correct course, because it is the common rule. Subjectively so long as you remain 'indifferent', whatever turns out will be full of grace... you see how, unwittingly, those whom you love and who love you best may come in the way of God's will. Many saints have found this out – you have to leave your nets and follow, you have to be quite alone, just as Christ was alone on the cross. It isn't easy. But is anything really easy when it is worthwhile. Blessed Henry Suso says 'if you would be everything to all men, turn yourself from all men' – that is your motto, and it is made up in a series of contradictions and paradoxes, just as the greatest mystics have been those, like St Bonaventure, St Teresa, St Catherine of Siena, whose lives have been fuller and more crowded by world affairs than any others.

Therefore, Jock, keep on in your life just as you are... I know it is easy for me to preach from the comfort and freedom of the Beda, with good holidays and my course nearly finished. But when I see the ease with which I have come this far, I realise I must be prepared to find abysses of sorrow and pain ahead, such as I have never dared contemplate. So it is with all spiritual life – it is purgative for a long and painful time. But it is worth it for the fruit of peace and joy it bears. Suffering is the key to love. Until we have suffered, and intensely, we can never love, intensely.

...Now you have gone through a good six months in Rome – the preliminary stage of God's plan. I do not say it has been easy for you, but it may have been easier than you had dared hope. Personally, I often find the trying time is in the evening, when one has shut one's door and have to work solidly till supper.

Well, God is very good and provides sweetness and comfort. But he does not do so for long, otherwise you would grow up a flabby, stodgy child. So He may take away your enjoyment – who knows? I am only warning you, because I don't know, and because I am scared of the spiritual 'lack-of-direction' in our seminaries. If it becomes a fact that you lose your interest, lose your love, lose your possibility of enjoying the Scots College – don't worry. Just keep on. It is God's testing time and he will not 'break the bent reed'.

You must excuse me writing like this. I have your future more at heart than I can say and leave you in the hands of God... Always remember the two little sayings which St Thérèse used to read so often. 'He loves us with an everlasting love' (from Jeremias I think) and the other from the end of Isias which I never can quote – something like 'as children carried at the breast, so will I comfort you.' Though to us it sometimes seems a slap in the face, it is really always a caress. We have only to try to do His will – and it is the trying that matters. Joys and sorrows can all equally well be offered up. Such is the love of God. Only we change. Please remember that I am always here and should always be free to see you. I admit any time that you have come I have been doing something else. But nevertheless do ask me if there is anything at all I can do. I feel I do not see half enough of you...

...Say a prayer for me sometimes. Tho' life is so full of joy, there are occasional problems and trials to be overcome, especially in the realm of study. But the comfort lies in the words of St Teresa of Avila; 'There is but one road which reaches God and that is prayer. If anyone shows you another, you are being deceived.'

Thank you for the joy of the last four days... and for always being so nice when we meet. ...I am going now to say a prayer for you after dropping this in at your door.

...PS I hope nothing in this will worry you. If it does forget it.

The next letter is undated, but probably written in late April. Michael has just returned from S. Giovanni Rotondo.

I am sorry I was not in – because I meant to tell you I wouldn't be, and was just too idle to come and do so. I have been gadding round Italy, as a matter of fact I went for a couple of days to see Padre Pio. The summer is always a time when I need particular strength – the Devil, world and flesh rush in as soon as I get away from here. Having had three days 'Heaven' I am now back…

It must have been either during this or one or two subsequent visits to Padre Pio that Michael enjoyed the 'enlightening' experience 'not open to many' of going into the monastery garden on a summer evening during recreation – which he described in *Hey, You!*

There, under the vines and among the cypresses, the Padre enjoys an hour or so of relaxation with those of the friars who are not busy and a few friends (one might say disciples), members of the Third Order. He is completely relaxed, the soul of the party. His interests are wide, ranging through politics and contemporary events to the number of Italians in London, his experiences in the army, the English cult of pets, the crops, the cost of living. He argues and is contradicted, he chaffs those sitting by, he takes snuff, passes it round, listens with interest to news and stories, is quick with repartee, has a lively sense of humour. Here I found a Gospel atmosphere, thinking again and again of the disciples clustered round Our Lord, questioning him, doubting his opinions, and not slow to voice their own, in no way quelled by magnificence but rather encouraged to talk by the humility and ready understanding of the listener. His whole attitude to life and to people is summed up again yet undefinably, as holiness. The effect is to radiate peace and joy; his face is alight: being with Padre Pio you can catch the eager begging of the apostles in the 'Lord, teach us to pray'. His fellow friars come by and pause to joke gaily; he is rebuked for having no faith in doctors; yet he is recollected in his light-heartedness. There is something about those evenings under the vines which lingers with you long afterwards, which perhaps does not die. But like all human things, there is an end, for the community has a bell and a routine, so Padre Pio says goodnight in the corridor with a smile, a blessing and a characteristic cuff on the side of the head with his mittened hand. (4)

Michael then responds to a request for advice from Jock as to how to respond to the negativity so often present in institutional life and the frustrations that accompany living in a critical atmosphere:

---

4 *Hey, You!*, (Burns & Oates, 1955), p119

Now for your question. You have struck a very difficult point. From personal experiences this is the worst time of the year for it, because it is hot and oppressive near the end of term and everyone is on edge with examinations. I think therefore one wants to be exceptionally careful just for those next few weeks not to increase the tension. That is only an immediate policy.

After this early example of his sensitivity as to the next step, he continues:

I think the general principles are something like this:

1) We must never be afraid (although I always am) saying what we mean when it is necessary. Our attitude is not to be ambiguous but quite clear cut. This means coming into bad odour quite possibly. It can only be adjusted by going on normally, treating people equally and nicely, even after a possible correction. But it takes time, and there is no hurry.

2) Silence is the best weapon. Argument seldom gets anywhere. But when there is occasion, you must speak your mind. It will only be tiresome for the 'general' public if it becomes a general nagging; so this must be avoided. Your attitude can well be anti-grumbling by silence, though it may seem slow and useless. If you build a reputation of 'Jock never grumbles', it will have its effect slowly. A practical way is to make an ejaculation for the person grumbling or something like that. As you know, when we are corrected, we often go in the other direction. When you have a 'born grumbler', it is not easy to correct him directly, but there is a chance of influencing others in the opposite direction.

3) In fact, grumbling is one of the most insidious diseases in a community, and can well effect a whole portion or a whole community even. Hence the prayer of the communist agitator. As with all things, there must be a personal approach – i.e. know your man. 'A' can be 'snubbed' and will take it and respond, but 'B' will harbour a grievance and not benefit.

4) In a seminary age doesn't count. That is you must respect a man's experience, but from now on, it is the soul that counts, and a child may teach the elders, so long as he is teaching God's love. This, of course, is unpopular. But if your conduct is otherwise normal and human it won't matter. In all things, it is the general way of life which gives the backing to your words – e.g. a priest who doesn't pray and has four hefty

meals a day doesn't win much of a following urging his flock to prayer and penance.

5)   Give yourself to prayer and the love of God. Anything that annoys is an excellent trial to offer in reparation for our faults and others. If you love God and cling to Him, you will learn when to correct openly and when in silence. I don't think there can be a perfect rule except

a) never grumble

b) never argue heatedly

c) try to associate happily with those who are most annoying

d) do all things for and in the love of God.

This is the way of the cross, but in its very bitterness it is full of joy; because LOVE is always giving, never wishing to receive and the more you desire to give, the more God will demand. There is no limit to this series – which is terrifying and overwhelming. But all the same, when we cannot any longer feel or even know that we are on the right track, we must believe and trust, because that is the greatest joy we can give for the Heart of Jesus, which thirsts for our sacrifices and our love.

…You are in my prayers. Don't overdo the exams. Health and a balance are more essential than these.

On May 10th, Michael writes his final letter of the seminary year, a summary of all he has tried to pass on to his cousin in the previous months.
It was lovely to see you last night, I am sorry I have nothing more interesting or comfortable to offer you when you come. Next year when I am promoted, you will have a chair to sit on, anyhow… You must understand when I talk that I have very little experience of spiritual matters. What is more I am very bad at talking and expressing myself, unless I have a definite line to go on. I am more used, in many ways, to talking in public than in private, though the latter is the only way for spiritual matters.

But I do want to say this:

1)   Your chief knowledge of the spiritual life will come from prayer, secondly, from spiritual reading, thirdly from a director. I'm not sure

whether this is the ideal order but I think it's the normal one today; there is not an abundance of good directors unfortunately.

2)   So long as you are striving after God, and fearing you are not getting anywhere, you are doing all right. Don't panic and don't over push; just keep going. It is when we sit back and get self-contented that we are slipping back and danger signals are showing.

3)   It is of the nature of advance that you see an increasing number of faults. It is like using a steadily bigger microscope, or gradually letting more light into a dark room.

4)   In prayer, the light – or closeness – of God gradually blinds the soul. I have heard it described like this: it is as if the soul gets out of focus in regard to God: this means there follows bewilderment and dryness etc., until you get into perspective again. There is probably in every soul's life a very long period of complete darkness, while all the little faults and bigger ones that prevent union with God are cut away and burnt out. Because of this sort of weedkiller process the soul of the person concerned seems dark and burnt up, and it is consequently painful. This is the time of faith and is of immeasurable value. It is also a time which reacts in the body and mind, so that it is a difficult period. I can't talk more in detail about prayer because I don't know how it goes with you. But if you ever feel the need, I can tell you what little I know.

5)   You will now be up to your eyes in work for the rest of the term. Somehow you must keep the main issue clear. You are here to save your soul, to become a saint, and then to sanctify others. Work is just incidental to this. Rightly applied it is a very big aid to union with God; wrongly, it is a distraction. So exams are to be worked for hard, but not to exhaustion, because they are only a means and not an end. But they can be sanctified by applying them to God's love for the holy souls.

6)   You are quite right about the presence of God. But the process is not very fast. We have to be faithful first to our set times of prayer which are the foundation of the whole building. They are the keystones of our bridge to God. The rest comes slowly. But we must be children at the start; in a way it's a game with God – how many times, in how many ways each day I can draw my mind to God, until the habit is built up.

Quite the most valuable and difficult is that each other person is a figure and image of God, to be loved with the greatest intensity. So often we find ourselves annoyed almost without thinking, by some tiresome habit, narrowness of outlook, idle word and such. It is tremendous training to marvel not in the weakness of those around, but in the fact they are not far worse. In this it helps to realise, as I am sure you do, that we are all apt to find a thing to criticise in another of which we ourselves are guilty. Somehow we have to bring everything back to God.

I find I behave quite childishly in my room sometimes – especially over things like cutting oneself shaving or breaking a bootlace etc., – if you laugh at yourself and thank God for such little trials, they all add up. We are often much too serious and could tend a hundred times a day to laugh with God at our own stupidity. So eventually we come to the realisation of Jesus within us, and when we adore the Blessed Sacrament, Jesus living in us loves his Eucharistic presence – God within us is loving and absorbing us in that love.

Once I begin I never can stop – and I am quite unqualified to write so. But it is hard to feel that there are such gaps in our lives and no one willing to fill them in. I don't know that you will get much out of those [commonplace?] books of mine. The writing is so very bad. But they always say such books show the lines a person's mind is running on. Perhaps at least you will find some one phrase which strikes you, and encourages you to read the work of the author concerned.

I really did enjoy my Sunday out 'on pilgrimage', and not least because I was able to see something of your Scots lads. It makes me feel very humble and wretched when I see what wonderful simplicity, enthusiasm and youth they are giving to the service of God. I must be getting old! At any rate, I love to meet them and gain a great deal from them…

…We had a most interesting talk from Mr Fred Copeland, ex-communist, leader of the Spithead naval mutiny, ex International Brigade in Spain and now a Catholic. I must tell you about it sometime.

PRESS ON!

Thin young priests: Michael and his cousin Jock Dalrymple, seated, with Dom Simon Trafford OSB standing
behind them, at Leuchie, Jock's home, 1955.

Michael's third year – and Jock's first – ended in June. Only one letter,
written in July, survives from the summer.

...So glad the holiday is a success. You can glimpse something of
what I call the 'unreality' of seminary life – it is hot house and intro-
verted, so that the frosts of living in public tend to nip the newly
ordained very much in the bud.

Accommodation, bringing the spiritual life into the daily life is essential
if we are to be seculars – as you say. We must still keep up a good lump
of specific prayer time as well, however you will find this means self-

74

mortification, as the only times usually not occupied are in the early morning. Uncle Hew will tell you this too.

Make the most of fresh air and exercise. We miss it terribly after an open life. But it is worth giving up anything and more for repayment of God's love…

Michael's first letter to Jock in the new seminary year, 1949-50, is written on the feast of Edward the Confessor, October 13th. Most of his letters are dated according to the feast of the day the letter is written – although changes in the liturgical calendar have meant several are now celebrated on different days.

Welcome back to Rome!

I have been praying hard for you in your retreat and hope that Our Lord has shown you his infinite mercy. So often, in fact always, it is impossible to measure 'success or failure' in a retreat. But if you played your part, the success is assuredly there.

Very soon now you will be swept into the 'Battle of the Books' – well, so be it. But let your other life go on, so that you study for the love of God and not for the sake of passing an exam.

Thank you so much for the day at the Villa. I loved it. You will be sorry in a way that it is over.

There isn't anything for me to say and I am particularly inarticulate at the moment. But I am sorry I made so little sense when we were talking about prayer. It is the old story which I find so hard to learn – I know nothing of these things, and it is only if by chance the H.G. [Holy Ghost] wants to use me as an instrument that any good will come. What can anyone know of prayer or say of prayer, really? There are a few do's and a few don'ts – but the only answer to any question is to keep on praying – what is praying – well keep on saying to God what you want to say – that you love Him, only you don't feel that you do; that you want to serve Him, only you always fail; that you want to pray but you can't – so there you are on your knees saying meaningless things over and over again while he smiles down on the efforts of his littlest one, and all the courts of Heaven burst into songs of joy.

Just keep on, Jock, and remember when you are not in chapel that the

lovely doctrine of the indwelling of the H.G. means we take God with us wherever we go – so that we can ask him always and all the time what we are to do next. Romans Ch. V & Ch. VIII are good on this. Be generous to God and learn to love – it is all that matters.
Pray that I may learn too.

His next letter is written three weeks later, on November 1st, the feast of All Saints; students from the Beda have just visited the Scots College, and Michael has been ordained a subdeacon.

… my only hesitation about yesterday was that it can't be much fun for you all to have large invasions of the Beda. It is so essential to keep happy relations as they have developed since we came back to Rome – but we don't want to abuse your kindness and hospitality. I'm probably over-fussy and stupid. But much good can come from a little Beda/Scots contact, but an overdose might ruin it all.

We staggered through the Mass today. Terence White as Deacon was superb, singing the Gospel really beautifully and doing all the ceremonies so carefully and reverently. Poor M.H. [Michael] did a very bad one-note Epistle, which can only be described as an act of love, because only a merciful God would accept such a wretchedness. He then muddled thro' to the end without actually dropping anything.

Thank you so much for the congratulations. The sub is a big step. For some 'the battle' comes at that time. God was kind to me and gave me the battle much earlier. This step was merely a cold hard act of faith and love and trust, because humanly there is no surety, no safeguard, no possibility of living up to the subdeaconship, let alone the priesthood. It is all very humbling and salutary. If it was not for a modicum of trust, I would have given up before now. As the time passes and all human things become more and more pressing and more and more unreal, you will find yourself thrown up on the hard rock of faith. And then there is no answering response… 'Jesus is asleep in my bark' – well let Him sleep then, because we are meant to live by faith and we can never have sufficient of it. Sometimes it is sweet to suffer, sometimes it is just humbling, sometimes it is very bitter. And perhaps the hardest and most common is the middle one…

So we keep on in smiling gaiety, living from one day to the next, not knowing how to get thro' with all that has to be done and knowing humanly we cannot, but (+ the grace of God) we shall be at the 'winning post' at the end of the race.

...But what fun it all is, and how I long for the day when I can congratulate you not only on the sub but on the Priesthood. Time telescopes and tho' looking ahead it may seem a long way off, spiritually you can never have sufficient time to prepare. It is all very wonderful, very consoling and impossible to understand or talk about. But I try to keep you in my prayers.

Looking forward to Saturday. Bring Stan Smith if you can, as Tony Farrar wants to see him – and as many others as you like – we had a party of nearly twenty a week ago in my room.

Michael writes again on November 24th, the feast – at that time – of St John of the Cross.

Jock's Ordination, July 11th 1954, with Michael returning from his parish in Soho to assist.

Have you got a cold? I meant to ask you. If so, take care. No risks in Rome: it's just not worth it.

I was talking to Fr King [Michael's confessor?] the other day about seminaries in general and confessors and we eventually came round to colleges in Rome and the impossibility of getting help when needed. He suggested that should you care to be put in touch with anyone who is 'on the right lines' and useful, he knows two or three in Rome, a couple of

J's [Jesuits] and a Franciscan I think, who might be of use and will be staying on more or less indefinitely. He also said that, of course, he is available for a few weeks, if you ever feel like a chat with him.

This is all awful cheek, because why should you talk to anyone? Quite, but I have always believed in following the example of the bee, and tho' not necessarily 'divulging one's whole life' – one can gain spiritually by sitting at the feet of holy men and just absorbing.

These suggestions are only thrown out. I don't know that you feel any particular need – but for what they are worth, give them a charitable interpretation and say a prayer for Michael.

The next letter, a brief one, is written on December 7th.

...Please laugh Boris out of being too tense before the Priesthood. He hasn't looked well this year and I told him so when I sent him a note the other day. The nervous strain is considerable and it looks as though it is wearing on him at the moment – there I am sticking my long nose in again. I beg especial prayers for myself – always needy, but at present more than ever. I have several, to me, very difficult Beda problems on hand at the moment.

The letter after this, written on what was then the feast of St Thomas, December 21st, includes the news of the death of Jock's old house master at Ampleforth, Stephen Marwood. Michael's comment on this is an example of two tendencies in his letters that often strike a jarring note for modern ears – an apparent negativity about this life and a constant belittling of his own efforts to live the gospel: '...however we are... in the hands of God and shall never really understand what He is doing to us until we get to Heaven – please God not a very long way off despite all our continual failings.'

That said, in his next letter, written on Christmas Eve, there is no sign of a 'vale of tears' spirituality, in fact, rather the opposite.

A very happy Christmas to you. May God shower down his graces upon you, so that you are filled with peace and joy... as we cannot be at home, God gives us the joy of being at the home of his Church, especially in this time of Jubilee. I do hope you will manage to see the functions well during this year, which may mean so much to the world, if it is carried through in a real spirit of pilgrimage, and not just in jollity. The pilgrims seem to be pouring in already...

...I don't know when I shall see you. Tomorrow, Sunday, I am due to be subdeacon at the Chiesa Nuova [the Church of St Philip Neri (1515-1595) who was another of the great formative influences on Michael] at 10.45 and shall be busy most of the day – perhaps we shall meet at S. Pietro on Monday. I am going to the Blue Nuns that morning for 48 hours pure rest, then on Wednesday I am taking two new boys down to Foggia [and Padre Pio] until Saturday which will miss your play I'm afraid...

...I am sorry to have seen so little of you lately, but life has been rather hectic in this part of the world. Things will be better now as my priesthood exam is over, and once the play is finished, life will be quieter.

Now I hope you are going to have a really merry Christmas – with lots to eat and drink – and plenty of fun and laughter... the time is such a lovely mixture of joy and peace – the season of Divine Poverty and of Divine Love; and most of all, of course, the time of childhood, when we can really become little and simple again. Remember that you can best show your love of God and your likeness to Our Lord at this time by giving yourself completely to others, as He gave Himself completely to us... keeping Him in mind when possible with little ejaculations of love, even in between mouthfuls of turkey and plum pudding – thinking that He loves to see us enjoying ourselves, and all the angels and saints and cherubs are leaning over the edge of Heaven, enthralled in our praise and glory of God as we sing carols or pull crackers, or whatever it may be – the world of spirits enjoying to the full all the human pleasures they had on earth, and the whole earth joining together in sun or snow or birdsong or anything else to bless the Lord.

... Keep a wee place for me between the plum pudding and dessert! I need prayers so urgently, and yours are of such value.

God bless you and keep you in his caress...

He writes again on the Feast of the Holy Name, January 1st, one of several letters in which he reflects with Jock on the spirituality of St Thérèse of Lisieux.

Michael begins with a reference to the annual play which traditionally the Beda, in common with other English speaking Roman seminaries, put on during Christmastide:

> Of course come! Heaven alone knows how many will be here – I shudder to think – so don't be late! I am supposed to be doing make-up and I don't expect I shall see much of you. But I have laid you on to have tea with Ted Conway, a very nice young Liverpudlian of 26, who was a bomber pilot in the war and who has just been home because his mother is seriously ill – but is recovering (which reminds me, Bobby Stuart's father died on Boxing Day. So say a prayer for his soul and get others to do the same. He was not a Catholic.)
>
> …Fr [later, Mgr] Gilbey asked after you, a charming man.
> Ref. St Thérèse… I haven't even seen it – the new book I mean – tho' Fr Vernon Johnson told me how good it was. I have the 'Definitive Biography' out of the library and will slip it you, if you like – none will know or care!
> I think perhaps Uncle Hew is a bit scared that you are too 'new' to St Thérèse to appreciate her letters which are the essence of her teaching perhaps! On the other hand, I have always been given to understand that if you want to know a person, it is best to read the letters rather than the 'works' – certainly so with St Bernard and people like that. I should not hesitate to 'dip into' the letters – though whether a close reading right thro' would be good, I don't know.
> It very much depends on you and how you get on with what you read – which is unpredictable even to yourself! Answer – try and see: if acceptable, go on; if not, don't drop St Thérèse but put the book aside till later. Frankly I have never read this definitive life! I'm never quite sure that 'biographies' give a very good picture, tho' they may help.
> I haven't wished you all I mean to wish and pray for 1950. Each day that passes brings us nearer to Heaven, which is a joy and consolation. Life develops more and more wonderfully, though how or why one cannot express. I am so intensely happy and so profoundly depressed! – well,

it's just an incredible paradox. But I do need your prayers and I do appreciate them. You have mine, constantly.

Leuchie [Jock's home] seem to have enjoyed Tony [Michael's brother], tho' poor Uncle Hew was hard hit by Fr Stephen's death.

Take care of yourself in this rather treacherous weather.

Any more news of their coming out at Easter?

The following week Michael writes a brief note to express his pleasure at Jock's news that his sister Elsie is coming to Rome for Michael's ordination on April 8th and adds: '…you may find some help in Romans 7 verse 14 onwards… keep praying for me but do not worry about bothering me. I have not broached spiritual things with you, because much is just keeping on until there is a problem. I am settled now to the last straight run of the race…'

The next letter is undated, and preceded by an additional note:

I enclose this which I have written in bits and disconnectedly in the past 24 hours.

I want to ask you one or two things about ordination if I can see you sometime… Perhaps you would like to come over one afternoon and watch me do Mass practice and criticise me…

The letter itself is the longest Michael wrote to his cousin and while composed in response to certain questions from Jock about the whole process of sanctification, is an excellent summary just before his priestly ordination of Michael's own spirituality at the time and all he had learnt in the previous four years. In the years to come he would maintain an enviable simplicity of faith and the same high degree of disciplined austerity in his own personal life, the latter initially part-mirroring the cold and hunger of post-war Rome and the narrower confines of the Church in the late forties. As time went on, however, he would become more tentative about urging this austerity on others – and instead, as his pastoral experience grew, develop an immense and very practical compassion, responding to each person and situation individually.

It's a terrific subject isn't it? And it will take the whole of life to solve. That is the first point. You see there is no hurry; although every minute is precious and not to be wasted, all the same, there is no hurry. Unless God has some very special plans sanctification will be your life work and will go on until the end. The battle never finishes and it is unlikely that even the greatest saints can go without sinning, unless they have reached the highest mystic union and even then they are probably not excluded from it – certainly not in any final sense. 'He that perseveres to the end...' – that is St Paul's hallmark of salvation.

...Well then, you have gone so far. Thank God for that. But is it not right that the first stages should be easier? It is like the description St Thérèse gives in her letter to Céline of the little child in its boat. You have been able to feel your progress and see your progress. Now perhaps it is the waves which attract your notice and you cannot appreciate how far away the shore is. At the same time the ocean is of infinite size and your human side sees that it has to go on and on and on. It feels a bit lost and despondent. Why not?

Added to this, there is nothing to mark your progress by – except failure. It is like sitting in a boat without oars, when the rollers seem to slide past you and every time you are just getting a view in the crest, you are in the trough again. But, if you have the oars, this doesn't justify your not rowing, nor does it mean that there is not progress. Simply that you cannot mark the progress. But who ever said that you should mark the progress?

What then have we got in the way of oars? Everything that happens in the day – and everything is good and bad. I'm sure St Thérèse got the essence of it here. It is anything done from the love of God – that is the only motive. All failure is a fall on our part. But rather than waste this fall, which can be so precious, we pick up the bits and give them to Jesus with a smile, and a word of sorrow – but we don't mope – we get on with the next act of love, and when that fails, do the same again. This is terribly revealing and terribly humiliating – and therefore very good for us. It is the wonderful antidote to our pride. We like to see ourselves doing things for God – but that is just what we can't do – we can only try and if we succeed it is by God's grace, and so we must thank Him for letting us do so. Unfortunately, if we often succeed, we forget to thank God, and begin to think we are fine fellows, which is nonsense.

Of course, your main question is – how do I do an act out of love of God and not out of love of myself for God? It is basic and if you can solve it, you are far advanced in sanctity. It is called many things – the practice of the presence of God, the Little Way, Holy Indifference, Self-Abandon to the will of God etc. But really it is the moulding of our whole personality, in our particular way, with the closest union with God. Only when our wills are perfectly conformed to his will, will we be sufficiently full of grace to resist all temptations. With Mary it was like that all her life – her fullness of grace assured her of never wavering. For us sinners it is a long and painful process – but we must not give up. We must be purged and the bitterest purgation is failure and striving for something we cannot attain. (To make paté de foie gras don't they tie the goose (!) to a stake and then chase it to enlarge the liver?). Not that God is chasing us (tho' He is, in the Hound of Heaven sense), but He has given us a glimpse of what we desire and then allowed us to be covered up again in the mire of our own baseness.

Don't you think that you are forgetting that all this is being done for God and as you say being upset because Jock who was coming on so nicely seems to be at a standstill or failing? But supposing God wants Jock to fail for this very reason? Then Jock must be content to fail, even till the end, just as Jesus failed on the cross. And by offering that failure he is offering the choicest gift to God, because we can have no satisfaction for ourselves in offering failure, and so we can only offer it out of pure love of God.

I suppose, quite frankly, the answer to your query how to love God every minute of the day is that you must be internally recollected. Now, don't think you have to be offering God everything at every minute, consciously. We would not be human. But if we can get to a state of recollection, we are never far from God and our hearts jump back to him. 'Where your treasure is, there is your heart also.' You know how someone you love fills your mind so that when you wake at night your mind is on him or her immediately, how he or she crops up on waking, at any spare moment, in the middle of a conversation. So it must be with God. I believe in inventing little ways to help oneself. They may or may not help you. St Thérèse says when you cannot pray or make a good act of love even, then you must do little things like smiling at someone, going out of your way to help, be nice or something, and give that as an act of love. Now I always carry my rosary loose in my pocket. (The light goes on and off and I am writing in semidarkness – excuse me). I put my hand in and at once tell the beads – going down the stairs or street I can say the rosary. I always say certain prayers while shaving in the morning, try to say an ejaculatory prayer on opening a door, etc. etc. These are my little makeshift things which can be increased and multiplied, or dropped according to their need or help. Mortification must be largely mental rather than physical in our present state. One can have a good, hard solid rule, but it is not wise to undermine one's strength too far, especially in this trying climate of Rome. Far harder and better mortification is in never losing your temper, being uncharitable, being distracted in chapel. I think to a certain extent you have to have bodily mortification to add to this and to aid it. One very good one practised by St Thérèse, was always obeying the bell, even in the middle of a sentence. It is a terrific mortification and one I fail to practise each time I come to tea with you. I am sure St Thérèse had some very set mortifications. We cannot afford to forget that her Little Way flourished inside a very strict rule. You might say it was the perfect keeping of that rule, especially in poverty, and the addition of perfection in her spare time, which made her a saint. But we can only follow her in principle – it is for each individual to work out his own details and, largely, it is by trial and error. The principle is make the most of all the things of the day – 'picking up a pin for the love of God' sums it up. To do this, our minds must be focussed on God, that our reactions might be 'God-ward' and not 'self-ward'. The elimination of 'I' and the substitution of 'Jesus' is the key. And failure and humiliation is the path. I don't think we can stress too much that we have to find a gift to offer God which has no appeal to 'self' – because it is fun offering a thing we enjoy. It is pride-satisfying offering a heroic act – but the heroism of love is offering the little things all the time especially when we don't enjoy doing so and feel unable to do anything good.

So when you feel sorrow for failure which is really self-pity, you must offer it to God with a smile and keep plodding on. The only way is that of the Cross.

Now it is very easy to become self-centred – don't I know it! All I do is done for me, not because I enjoy it or because it makes me good in my own eyes. We must fight this positively by looking more at God then. Prayer is very essential, because it helps recollection; it does not matter what sort of prayer, but it will inevitably be simplified all the time. On the whole, it is safe to say anything too complicated is barking up the wrong tree, either in prayer or mortification, because we interest our-selves in the prayer or mortification, and not in the pleasing of God. So no 'stunts' just plodding and pin-pricks.

As regards the narrow and broad mind. It is very perplexing and diffi-cult; it is only worthwhile laying down the law if you are going to effect something by that; otherwise it only annoys and perhaps shuts the door to further progress. Patience is the watchword of humility – I find myself in continual disagreement with those I like best and admire most – well, I must accept it humbly, have my own opinion but don't ram it down the throats of others – perhaps they aren't made to like it.
This is very rambling and probably useless... It depends if I have been humble enough to let the H.G. and not Michael play the tune. At any rate, the summary seems to me not to worry, not to look at your faults but the mercy and love of God, and then to go plodding on, not expecting any-thing of progress, but avoiding backsliding – pray for poor Michael.

This letter is undated – and no other letters survive or were written till after Michael's priestly ordination. All we have for this period is one sen-tence in *Living Priesthood*: '...during the diaconate, oddly enough, I had more strain than at any other time and with the rector's permission fled to the solitude and peace of Assisi.' (5) We also know that almost in defer-ence to the way at different times throughout the four years at the Beda he had leant towards the contemplative life, he did his pre-ordination retreat in the Trappist Monastery of Tre Fontane, just outside Rome.

Michael was ordained priest by Archbishop Traglia, on April 8th, 1950 at the Basilica of St John Lateran. The ceremony
commenced at 6.30 am, and ended around 2 pm. It was long, hard, glorious, triumphalist, splendid and something I would not have missed

---

5 *Living Priesthood*, (McCrimmons, 1991), p22

for the world. In a way it was the climax to the long hours each day I had spent alone in prayer. I was not just alone there with God, but had now been brought to the position, function, office or anything one wants to call it, which left me committed – as I had first thought I was meant to be – to people. Tre Fontane offered something beautiful, deep, attractive but distant. I had lived the life and death of incarnation in World War II, and for me reality in all its joy and pain remained in the heart of the world. (6)

Among those present at the ordination were Michael's sister Sylvia, his brother Tony, his cousin Elsie with her old Nanny, Nanny Waters, and an Ampleforth monk, Fr James Forbes, (no relation to Michael's former army chaplain and inspiration, George). From St John Lateran, they all trooped to Piazza Navona, and lunch in a restaurant known as 'The Pope's Grandfather', its founder apparently having cooked for Pope Benedict 13th. They sat down at 3pm and rose at 8.30pm – 'a memorable meal in a wonderful atmosphere', according to Elsie Gibbs.

The next day Michael celebrated his first Mass with the Blue Nuns [the Little Company of Mary], and then he and his guests attended the Holy Year High Mass in St Peter's, before setting off for Assisi by train. They visited the Portiuncula, the Carceri and San Damiano, and Michael said his second Mass in the Lower Church of San Francesco. Although she commented that, characteristically, Michael 'never said much', Elsie Gibbs recalls it as a time of wonder, while for Tony Hollings it was four days of 'blissful joy and happiness.'

The following week, April 19th, Michael is writing to Jock, with a gift.

I enclose a relic of St Thérèse as a thanks offering for all your kindness over this ordination period.

I fear that is not an *ex ossibus* [from the bones] relic, as these are extremely difficult to get, but it is quite a good relic for all that. I feel sure that if your devotion to the Saint grows, you will find her a very wonderful counsellor and friend in Heaven – and that is where our strength comes from in all we have to do on earth.

God bless you and thank you immensely for all you have done.

6 Ibid, pp22-23

A number of short notes follow. In one in early May he writes 'I am going to try to go to say Mass at Cassino on Thursday, if I can summon the energy to get the train', and a week later reports on 'a wonderful day' at the monastery whose destruction he had witnessed only seven years earlier.

On 19th June, he writes a final letter from Rome, consoling Jock over an undivulged disappointment.

My last Beda note.

I was so sorry for you this evening that I thought I would write this line before I went to bed.

I think I can truly say that I know what you are feeling to some extent and I go through it myself. Frankly, there is nothing to relieve the position, because it is largely our human side. We think we see clearly what would be a good thing for ourselves, others – the Church in general – then the opposite occurs for no seeming reason and we get het up and depressed about it. I think we shall find it much more in parishes and we have to so unite our whole selves to God that we can know automatically when to put up with a situation and when to oppose it – because of His will and not ours.

In this particular case, you must try to see only God's will, even tho' it seems a 'misdirected' will. It often happens – God permits it and the thing works out for the best in the end. But it leaves us feeling small and very frustrated and generally upset.

This, of course is a good thing because it makes us a little humble and a little more dependent on God and not on ourselves. If we can have a keynote of confidence, based upon love – then we go on unshaken. As St Thérèse liked to quote from Job – 'Tho' thou shouldst kill me, still will I hope in thee'. You know all this better than I can say it – I will only add that God has allowed this blow at this time for a very particular reason and if you accept it with your will, though your human feelings etc. rebel, then He can make the most of the opportunity. It is not easy, but He will help.

Good luck in the last exam – love to all Scozzeze. Say a prayer for me in my need. Till Lisieux… God bless you, Michael.

After time with Jock in Lisieux, Michael crossed the channel. In *Living Priesthood*, he describes the beginning of the rest of his life.

> There was little contact with or from the Diocese during four years in Rome. Perhaps it was for this reason that I thought I had been forgotten on my return to England. After several weeks I wrote and asked for work and the then Vicar General sent me to St Patrick's, Soho Square, in the centre of London's West End.
>
> St. Patrick's presbytery was dilapidated, as were the Rector and the two housekeepers. On my arrival, I was sent up to the first floor, and found the ancient, almost blind, and delightful Parish Priest seated behind his desk. Without his getting up, or my sitting down, he greeted me with a five minute interview, the burden of which was: 'There's nothing to do here. I look after the school; the other priests look after the hospitals. Well I expect you'll find something. Good afternoon!' (7)

Jock Dalrymple is a nephew of his namesake, Fr Jock Dalrymple, and a first cousin, once removed, of Michael Hollings. Like Michael, he studied at the Beda College in Rome, although like him very much at the youthful end of the Beda spectrum. He is now parish priest of a newtown parish in the Kingdom of Fife, St Paul's, Glenrothes and St Mary, Mother of God, Leslie.

---

7 Ibid, p23

CHAPTER FOUR

Michael Hollings at Oxford

RODERICK STRANGE

I first heard about Michael Hollings when I was studying for the priesthood in Rome in the nineteen sixties and I quickly became irritated. Fellow students who had been undergraduates at Oxford seemed to talk about him constantly. It was 'Father Michael this' and 'Father Michael that'. I found it rather tiresome and I remember thinking that unless I met him soon, I would start to dislike him. Then he was invited to give the community retreat at Palazzola, the English College villa, in the autumn of 1969.

I cannot recall our first meeting, but various incidents from that week remain in my mind. I remember Michael's ease with us: 'I'm not too good with handles,' he said and so 'Father Michael' became 'Michael'. I remember his frankness. As part of the retreat, each of us newly ordained deacons led a Holy Hour. Mine was much appreciated by Michael, but he nevertheless told me that its fluency was too polished: 'If you preach like that, Rod,' he said, 'I wouldn't want to listen to you every week.' Then there was his generosity. I had been accepted as a graduate student at Oriel College Oxford for the following autumn, but an anomaly in the law at that time meant that I could not apply for a grant. Michael knew that money would be tight; he approached me quietly in the garden one day and handed me an envelope with the comment, 'This is from a legacy I've just received', and I found myself with a cheque for a hundred pounds – a very princely sum in those days. A phrase he used during one of the retreat sessions has stayed with me and I have often used it since with others: 'There's a lot of talk these days about finding Christ in others, but the burning issue is [that was the expression he used, "the burning issue"], will they be able to find Christ in you?'

I was ordained priest that December in England and visited Oxford in the January to make arrangements for going up to Oriel later that year. I stayed at the Old Palace, which is the residence at the heart of the Chaplaincy. The temporary buildings, put up after World War II, had just been demolished in preparation for the erection of new ones. It was the feast of the Epiphany and Michael invited me to say the midday mass, which had to be celebrated in his room. It was the largest space available and was packed. Unfortunately he had forgotten to leave me the book with the Prefaces to the Eucharistic Prayers. I had no idea where it was and the room was too crowded for anyone to go and search. It was an early experience of improvisation. He was amused when told. There was no need to be too polished!

That day is also memorable for me because we were joined at lunch – a typically large gathering – by a couple who had driven down from Yorkshire to visit. Frank and Mary Ashby were close friends of Michael's. They were making plans to move to Oxford to help administer the developments at the Chaplaincy which Michael was organising. They became my close friends too. Part of Michael's gift was to spread friendship.

I lived at the Chaplaincy for sixteen of the next nineteen years. Beginning in October 1970 I was there for four years as a graduate priest, assisting the chaplains when invited to do so, returning in July 1977 as a chaplain myself. Michael had left Oxford in the summer of 1970, but the style of Chaplaincy life which he had created was continued and developed by his successor, Fr Crispian Hollis, who is now the Bishop of Portsmouth. Crispian, with Professor Barry Nicholas as Chairman of the Newman Trustees, assisted by Frank Ashby, had the particular responsibility of overseeing the construction of the new Chaplaincy buildings. Father (now Monsignor) Walter Drumm was Crispian's assistant from 1973, succeeded him, and maintained the tradition. I became Walter's assistant in 1977 and in turn succeeded him in 1983. When I came to leave in 1989, it was thirty years since Michael had arrived as Chaplain. Michael,

Crispian, Walter and I are four very different people, but we nurtured a way of living in that Chaplaincy which, while it remained coherent, developed and grew. Michael had supplied the vision.

Michael in the Chaplaincy

One of the features which people tend to identify most readily with in that vision is the fact that it was an open house. The origins of this policy lie in Michael's early days as a priest. When he was newly ordained he felt ashamed by the way the lunch hour in his first presbytery was sacrosanct – no phone calls were allowed or doorbells answered. It bred in him 'a determination somehow, at whatever cost, to open any place where I had some authority'.[1] The Oxford Chaplaincy was the first place in which he was able to do that.

---

1 *Living Priesthood.* McCrimmons, 1991. p25.

Michael with students in the Old Palace

Doors were unlocked at 7.00 in the morning and locked around midnight. Details of that changed, especially in later years when there were more students living in the building and the particular demands of security became more urgent, but the principle of openness remained. It was not always an easy option, but it bore fruit. Undergraduates were not left undisturbed in isolated privilege. If they popped in for breakfast or tea, as they often did, they might find themselves chatting to almost anyone; sometimes a distinguished guest invited to speak to one of the Chaplaincy societies, or possibly Michael Casey or David Phillips or Peter Lister. For those who remember, these are names to conjure with. Many others could be added. But one point that needs to be stressed is the way openness was not softness, nor did it collapse into chaos. Michael's tradition was also tough. He had authority. To repeat a remark made more than once before, he had not been a Major in the Coldstream Guards for nothing. People were not allowed to take everything for granted. They could be shown the door firmly and indeed forcibly. And sometimes they were.

But it was not only the policy of the open house that Michael put into operation in Oxford. Here at last he had the opportunity to be a leader again, not now as a soldier but as a priest. I have realised this fact properly only recently and by chance. I was checking a reference for something entirely different in the library here at the Beda College in Rome where Michael was a student and where I am now rector, and came across an article, written by Michael for the *Beda Review* at about the time of his ordination in March 1950. It is the text of a talk he had given in the college and it is called, 'Some Notes on Leadership'.[2] Very little is dated. For so young a man he speaks with extraordinary authority. The experience of war underpins what he writes. As I read, I recognised the Michael I would come to know twenty years later.

He concentrates on three things. The first, he said, was humility, because 'to lead, a man must be whole and human; he can only really be human if he is humble, because he can never have full confidence in himself unless he knows how very limited are his capabilities'.[3] An essential corollary to this recognition of limitations, he argued, is a readiness to trust others and work with them. And the Chaplaincy style which Michael exercised and developed was based upon encouraging undergraduates to use their own talents. He gave them the freedom to do that.

An outstanding example of that policy was the origin of the Oxford Lourdes Pilgrimage. Soon after he became Chaplain, Michael was approached by two undergraduates, Tim Firth and Michael Kenworthy-Browne, who asked about the possibility of starting a specific University pilgrimage to Lourdes. Michael himself already went to Lourdes regularly and, in fact, was there when he heard the news of his appointment to Oxford. And so the Oxford Pilgrimage to Lourdes began. It takes place still, now in alliance with Cambridge. At the beginning, and throughout my time in Oxford, a group would go from the University each year, not

---

2 'Some Notes on Leadership' in the *Beda Review*. March 1956, pp20-27.
3 Ibid. p21.

taking those who were sick, but going to work with the sick as brancardiers and handmaids. Those who came were not only current undergraduates, but also former members of the University. It became something of an unofficial annual reunion. We worked hard, we had wonderful parties and we soaked up the atmosphere of faith, prayer and service which is intrinsic to that place. After his own time as Chaplain had ended, Michael would still come, guiding and encouraging by his readiness to undertake the most demanding tasks. He only stopped coming when he could no longer work. That spirit of service to those in need, symbolised by the week in Lourdes and the reunion in mid-February, was a characteristic element of Chaplaincy life, but it happened first of all because Michael welcomed the initiative that others were taking.

Blessing a car outside the Old Palace

In the Chaplaincy in general, activities did not revolve around the possibility of his presence. In due course so much was going on that it would have been completely impossible in any case. By the time I was Chaplain, there were occasions when four or five meetings were taking place simultaneously. The readiness to work with others and to delegate was the key.

Michael's observations on delegation lead to his second point, courage, 'because', as he observed, 'it often takes courage to delegate or to assume a new task'.(4) The courage he meant is not flashy, glamorous or extrovert, but is perhaps best understood when seen in partnership with fear. It was a lesson learnt in war. As he was to say later, 'I learnt that if you have cowardly instincts as I do, the only hope is to face the fear, the unknown, the threat.'(5) The context for courage can take unusual forms. It will involve taking risks and being prepared to suffer the anxieties, or even terror, which that course of action entails. Consider finance. When Michael was appointed Chaplain, he was the first in Oxford not to have had private means or at least some way of supporting himself. In his book *Living Priesthood* he speaks of having to make at least a couple of thousand pounds each year to keep the Chaplaincy going. He describes it as a nagging grievance, but admits that it forced him to maintain a variety of interests which he enjoyed, giving talks and retreats, writing books and continuing the television advisory work which he had begun earlier.(6) He does not, however, mention another equally significant activity which Professor Barry Nicholas recalled in his address at the Memorial Mass for Michael which was celebrated at the Chaplaincy in May 1997. He was speaking of Michael's determination to make the whole financial situation at the Chaplaincy much more stable.

Professor Nicholas explained that soon after Michael had begun his work as Chaplain, the building immediately to the south of the Old Palace, which houses Alice's Shop and the Restaurant Elizabeth, came on to the market. Michael suggested that the Newman Trust, which then as now owned the Old Palace, should raise or borrow sufficient money to buy the property and refurbish it, so that it could become an asset for the

---

4 Ibid. p23.
5 *Living Priesthood*, p.20; & see 'Some Notes on Leadership', p23.
6 *Living Priesthood*, p34.

Chaplaincy. Professor Nicholas continued, 'But the Trustees, of whom I confess I was one, felt that the risks involved were too great.' What did Michael do? 'He said no more, but went off and raised the necessary funds himself. Then, when he had refurbished the building, he gave it to the trustees.'(7) And what a valuable asset that purchase has proved to be. This story, raised a warm smile among the congregation at the Memorial Mass. It illustrates Michael's generous nature and shows his exceptional pragmatism. Professor Nicholas commented, 'Over the years I came to think that, had he not been called to the priesthood, he could have been a very successful entrepreneur.' But it also displayed his courage. The risks foreseen by the Trustees would have been as clear to Michael, but he decided to press on. He acted on his own, knowing he would be accountable for what he was doing. Two of the elements involved here – loneliness and taking responsibility – had been mentioned by Michael in his *Beda Review* article as crucial aspects of courage.(8)

It is worthwhile pausing here to stress the practical side of Michael's nature. Some of those who did not know him personally have acknowledged his high ideals but have tended to suggest he was impractical. Nothing could be further from the truth. Michael was consistently aware of the practical implications of his plans. For example, besides the particular episode recalled by Professor Nicholas, he also set up the St Thomas More Housing Trust, a housing project for overseas students, who were coming to Oxford in increasing numbers in the nineteen sixties. At that time most colleges could not accommodate them all as they had not yet embarked on the building developments which became such a feature of the eighties and nineties. This scheme was both generous to those in need and helped to give the Chaplaincy greater financial security.

Those same gifts were in evidence again before Michael left the Chaplaincy. There was a clear need to replace the temporary buildings I

---

7 Barry Nicholas, Address given at a Memorial Mass for Fr Michael Hollings at the Oxford Catholic Chaplaincy, 21 May 1997, typescript, pp1-2.
8 'Some Notes on Leadership', pp24-5.

mentioned earlier with something more permanent. The building cost £250,000, which today would be about five million, but there were no funds. 'Everything had somehow to be raised,' to quote Professor Nicholas again, recalling the 'boldness of the step' that Michael took in finding the money. That building and the care Michael took to give the Chaplaincy financial stability have been a source of blessing on the lives of his successors and countless other members of the University for whom it has been a spiritual home. Realistic practicality was a means to an end, to free people so that they could come to know, love and serve the one true God and Jesus Christ, whom he had sent, and so spend themselves in the service of others. That was the essential business.

Unsurprisingly, therefore, Michael's third note on leadership concerns generosity, which he says is 'coterminous with charity'.[9] It calls for an enthusiasm which does not count the cost. The leader must lead from the front, not the middle or the rear. Michael's leadership is most clearly seen in his dedication to prayer. It is difficult to illustrate such a commitment and its influence.

Michael himself, of course, was known to rise early and to pray for long hours. He speaks in *Living Priesthood* of learning this lesson and training himself in this self-discipline at the Beda.[10] He became a distinguished teacher about prayer, a director and a guide. As Chaplain he gave talks on prayer and later he would sometimes come back and speak by invitation. Two of his remarks particularly remain with me. The first touched on the personal character of prayer. He said he was quoting St John of the Cross, although I've never checked the reference, to the effect that no two people go more than halfway along the same road to God. Some of the way we travel together, that is why we can talk about it and support one another, but a part of the journey is always unique to each person. The second remark was his observation that 'prayer is addictive, but the hangover comes first.'

---

9 Îbid., p25.
10 *Living Priesthood* pp20-1.

Beyond the teaching, however, was the example. When I first went to the Chaplaincy, Michael had already moved to Southall, but a good half hour before the early Mass each morning, a fair number of people would be gathered in the chapel, praying silently, preparing themselves for the Mass and for the coming day. They were there because of Michael; they were following his example. While I cannot attribute my own commitment to prayer simply to Michael, because that was made before I was ordained, neither can I underestimate the benefit to me, as a newly ordained priest, of finding myself in a setting in which that habit of lengthy prayer at the beginning of the day was well established and taken for granted.

Michael had left Oxford the term before I arrived, so these reflections do not come from my immediate experience. Others whom he served as Chaplain can speak more directly. I have been speaking, rather, of the effects of his ministry and trying to trace them to their source. Nevertheless, during my time he visited regularly, though not often. He did not intrude, but he was always interested in developments. He would come to preach when invited, he continued as a Trustee of the St Thomas More Housing Trust and kept up the Lourdes connection. Sometimes he would stay with the Ashbys for a couple of days to combat excessive tiredness and that would be an opportunity for a meeting, an exchange of news and ideas, and cheerful celebration: Frank and Mary's hospitality was always a definition of generosity.

I last met Michael in February 1995. I had been invited to work for a day with priests and catechists of the Westminster Diocese on the Rite of Christian Initiation for Adults (RCIA). Michael came at lunchtime. I think he had had a wedding in the morning. He hobbled in, very lame, and looked aged and unwell. Had he come to support me, or would he have come in any case? I don't know. It makes no difference. Characteristically, he was there.

Later, when there were allegations brought against him, he had to absent himself from the parish. I wrote to him and he, punctilious in correspondence as ever, scribbled a reply. Soon he was able to return, but I was busy with other things. I heard that he had died, but only afterwards did I learn of his declining health and the surgery. Now I think about Michael's dying.

At the heart of the Gospel is a message of faithful love, the faithful love of Jesus for his Father and for us. It was an unconditional love, love without reserve. Our calling as his disciples is to reflect that love in our own lives. Such fidelity, we believe, will receive its reward. And it will. However, Michael's dying teaches that such a reward may not be foreshadowed in this life. Michael was not perfect – he would have poured scorn on the notion – but if ever a man strove to be faithful to the Lord, it was Michael. I do not know the deathbed scene, but the process of dying was marked by accusations, declining health, amputation of a leg, coma, and final passing away without regaining consciousness. Perhaps Michael's final gift to me is the lesson that those who follow the Master may be asked to die in darkness. For that gift and all the many others, I give thanks.

Roderick Strange is a priest of the Shrewsbury diocese who studied at the English College in Rome, with further studies at Oxford following his ordination. In 1977 he returned to the University as Chaplain. He is currently the Rector of the Beda College.

CHAPTER FIVE

Chaplain and Counsellor

SHEILA CASSIDY

Michael Hollings remained until his death my Number One ecclesiastical hero, guide, philosopher, friend and role model. When we first met, in the Somerville College Infirmary in 1960 or 61, it was, on my part, love at first sight. I couldn't quite register that this tall and gentle priest had actually come to see me because he cared about me, although we had never met.

At that time I was in my second year at Oxford, having transferred from the University of Sydney where I had begun studying medicine in 1956. The Catholic Chaplain during my first year was Father Valentine Elwes, an elderly, extremely distinguished priest who, not unreasonably, kept his distance from the students. I remember to this day that the Chaplaincy card declared that Father Val would see students by appointment: I wonder how many took up that offer? I don't think I did. It's not that he wasn't kindly – just that students tend to have their crises out of normal working hours and when they need help are inclined to need it now.

Michael was very different. In that first autumn term of 1960, he declared the Chaplaincy an 'open house' and we took him at his word, coming to breakfast, lunch and tea, no doubt eating and drinking him out of house and home. I have such vivid memories of those days: the taste of corn-flakes and boiled eggs at breakfast after Mass and the feel of the brown loaf as I cut it to feed students endless rounds of bread and jam for tea. I remember the kettle behind the screen next to the drinks cupboard, the red of the cushions on the window seats and the sight of Michael's cloak spread over the chair behind his desk. I remember the slope of the floor and the blackened wood of the Old Palace and the sound and intonation of Michael's voice answering the phone: 'Four-Seven-Eight-Seven-0.'

Sheila Cassidy at a book launch

In those halcyon undergraduate days, the Chaplaincy became the centre of my world. I would leave my bedsit in Blackhall Road or, later, my flat at 143 Walton Street, around 7.30 in the morning and cycle through the town and down the hill towards the Chaplaincy in time to attend the 7.45am Mass.

Some time soon after he arrived in Oxford, I cottoned on to the fact that Michael prayed before Mass. As my love for God (or was it for Michael?) grew, I arrived earlier and earlier in order to sit in silence with him. I tried coming five minutes early, then ten, then fifteen and eventually half an hour or more, and would sit patiently on the wall outside the chapel until he opened the door at about 7.00 or ten past. Then I would take my seat on the right-hand of the chapel and try to pray, sneaking glances, the while, at Michael's figure in the sanctuary, to the right of the altar, wrapped up in his great woollen cloak.

Once settled, he would not move until it was time to prepare for Mass, so I too would sit or kneel as quietly as I could, trying to pray and wondering how he did it, i.e. how he actually prayed. I know now that he was just sitting, keeping company with God, as St Irenaeus puts it, in rather the same way that mystics of all religions pray: without words, without images, without desire: content just to sit, empty before God. Prayer, of course, was Michael's life source, the fount from which he drank deeply each day, the origin of the love and compassion which he poured out upon us students and, for years to come, upon the various poor who flocked to his house each day.

Michael at forty was an enchanting personality, perhaps more tolerant than in his later years, or perhaps as Chaplain he saw it as his job to be there for the students, round the clock, in *loco parentis* and more. My first memories of him as comforter were when I was brought to him broken-hearted at the news that the student I thought I loved was engaged to be married to someone else. I don't recall what he said, merely that he was there: the obvious person to turn to in times of distress. I think I knew, even then, that Michael was the sort of man to whom one could go with any kind of problem. He was the type of man to whom sinners could instinctively turn without fear of being sent packing: I always knew that I could go to him whatever I had done. As things have turned out for me, I have never been unwittingly pregnant, fallen foul of the law or been smitten with AIDS, but I know that if something like that had happened, I should have gone straight to Michael.

Having said that, I should add that Michael did not suffer fools gladly and I myself learned to be a little wary of him with the passing years after I experienced the sharp end of his tongue.

What Michael provided for the students was what psychotherapist John Bowlby called a Secure Base: a place of safety to which we could run if we were distressed, confused or lonely and from which we could move away to explore the world. If this seems a rather childish notion, perhaps we forget just how young some undergraduates are, both chronologically and emotionally. In the early sixties, many young Catholics, including myself, had come to Oxford straight from boarding school or from home and almost certainly from single sex-schools, so the Chaplaincy provided a place for us, emotionally inexperienced as we were, to meet and make friends, as well as a place for us to lick our wounds when things went wrong. At one stage I almost lived there, installing myself with my sewing machine in Michael's large sitting room and making bright coloured trousers for the summer and a gown of blue furnishing satin for an important dinner at high table. (I remember, too, that the long zip at the back, hastily tacked in, came apart at some vital moment!)

102

My social life, like that of many others, was based around the Chaplaincy, and the mid morning Mass on a Sunday was the great meeting point of the week. An enthusiastic cook and entertainer, I would gather up a dozen or more students who had no previous commitment and invite them to my flat for lunch. Having collected half a crown from each guest I would cycle off to the corner shop and buy the ingredients for spaghetti bolognese or tuna risotto and have lunch ready for them when they arrived. Sitting on the floor, we would eat off our laps and spend the next few hours talking as only students can. My memory is that we spoke of things religious – I was never interested in politics and, at that time, would not have known the meaning of the expression Human Rights. I have no recollection of being concerned for the poor in those days: my passion was only for the sick and for Catholicism.

I wish now that I had had an adult's friendship with Michael, but he was not an easy man to know closely. Sometimes – probably quite often, he seemed impatient of his well-off, middle class disciples from the past, for there was no doubt that in later years, he had thrown in his lot with the poor. In Michael's house, the poor were a bit too close for comfort. He was always hospitable to me and there was a time when I stayed with him whenever I was in London. Doris, his faithful friend and housekeeper, would make up a bed for me wherever there was room and there was always time to touch base with him in his office – his only bit of personal space. One night I was given a room on the second floor and was seriously unnerved when, on the way back from my bathroom, two young men burst in through the fire escape and ran down the corridor. I locked myself in my room and tried to sleep, only to be kept awake by their loud, angry quarrelling in the next room.

Michael was the heart of St Mary's and it was bliss to be welcomed by him when I arrived late at night from Paddington. Sometimes, however, he was out talking or dining with friends and then the house felt terribly bleak with one or two silent men or women slumped on the battered chairs in the dining room watching the television. It was hard not to feel petulant and cheated that the sparkling wits of yesteryear had moved on and that Michael's family then was a very wounded one. Now, as the millennium draws to a close and I complete my training as a psychotherapist I recognise what a haven Michael's home must have seemed for those whose childhood neglect or abuse had deprived them of normal social graces and friends. I suppose, with hindsight, St Mary's was a sort of therapeutic community and it is small wonder that I felt a little uncomfortable if Michael was not there to protect me.

I learned too, as the years went by, that Michael had no time or heart for spiritual talk with the well-off. My private times with him were brief and always punctuated by phone calls. Michael had the therapist's gift of undivided attention and I probably learned more from hearing him talk to distressed people on the phone that I did from personal counsel. And yet it was always so good to be there with him in that room, with Thomas his old tabby cat and the black cloak and the ever cluttered desk.

There are some men or women who are icon figures: who become somehow translucent, so that being with them feels like being on holy ground. Michael was one such man; Jean Vanier is another. It is a privilege to enter their chaotic space, and to sit briefly in the eye of their stormy world. As I get older, I realise that I have heard all the spiritual counsel – indeed, I can give it myself. The importance is not in the speaking but in the doing and, of course, the doing is messy because wounded people are messy. Michael's people were the poor, the homeless and those who were in trouble with the law. Mine are the sick – cancer victims of every age and class – while Jean's are the mentally handicapped. No work is better than the other – one does what one can, according to one's gifts and strengths and wherever the spirit leads. I would be no good in Notting Hill and worse at L'Arche, but I move with grace and joy through the wards and corridors of a great hospital.

The problem with putting people on pedestals is that when they do something purely human, others get scandalised. But perhaps the scandal is

104

important because it throws the ball of holiness or good works back into the admirer's court. The true fruits of my hero worship for Michael are what I do for others, not my ongoing admiration of him. As I wrote earlier, there was a moment in which I caught the sharp end of Michael's tongue and I never really felt entirely safe with him again. It happened when I was in my thirties and on a trip back from Chile. My life had been so changed by the coup there against Allende and my experience of 'real' poverty, that I longed to tell Michael about it. I came to stay for a few days at Southall where he was parish priest and waited impatiently to be invited for a tête-à-tête. It was three days before he would see me and I was devastated to be told that I had been so full of my own talk about Chile that I had been blind to the various shades of poor right under my nose in his house. It was reminiscent of an occasion when I was a child and my father, irritated by my discourteous behaviour, woke me from sleep and beat me for being rude to some important guests. I suppose you could say that Michael woke me from my sleep of adolescent hero-worship with a verbal cuff around the ears, but I was too immature, even in my thirties, to understand what I had done. I understand it now, of course, but it hurt for years.

Most of the time, however, he was wonderfully patient, but I recall how churlish he was one evening, just a few years before he died, when I took him out to dinner. I see now that he was tired, irritated and in pain and he probably didn't really want to go out to supper with me when he had urgent things he had to do. He was complaining of his diabetes and his feet and I passed on to him a tip from an old diabetic specialist friend of mine: that he should change his shoes several times a day to change the areas of pressure on his feet and lessen the risk of ulcers. I realise, even as I write, that he probably had only one pair of shoes while I took it for granted that he would have several. Anyway, he snapped at me that he hadn't asked for my advice and that I was not his doctor. So that was that and after a rather awkward supper together he went back to his desk while I went sadly on my way.

As I got older and, no doubt, more fussy about my creature comforts, I found other London friends to stay with and stopped going to St Mary's. We still spoke on the phone and I could see him, in my mind's eye, sitting at the cluttered desk, with his cloak draped over the chair. That cloak became a symbol of my relationship with Michael – a shared joke and a relic of days when we were younger and less caught up in the pain of the real world. It was when Michael was Chaplain at Oxford and I had the flat at 143 Walton Street. He was in his thirties, I around twenty-four. I was going to a ball – I can't remember where – and had decided that I needed a long black cloak, i.e. Michael's cloak, to complete my ensemble. Michael gave permission, with the proviso that I should line it with scarlet. I readily agreed and my medical student friend Eleanor and I spent many happy hours with the massive cloak (Michael was a tall man) spread out on the floor, pinning and then sewing the scarlet lining. The result was stunning and the material lasted for the next thirty years, as far as I know.

One of the really good things about Michael, in those bigoted years, was his openness to people of other beliefs. Eleanor, if I remember rightly, was an agnostic and my Chilean friend Consuelo, whom Michael subsequently met, was an atheist. Now, in my own more agnostic and questioning years, I really miss the opportunity to bounce ideas off him. Michael was always ahead of his time in terms of liturgical reform and had none of that pomposity about Catholicism that I find so alienating in some clergy.

Once again, this is why I miss him so much. I want to laugh with him, now that I can see the simplicity of the gospel message so clearly, the stark and terrible clarity of Christ's teaching on love, forgiveness and justice. 'Love one another', he said, 'as I have loved you.' Michael did just that, so that he became Christlike, the saint of Notting Hill. But although he lived in Christ and Christ in him, he was a man, a frail human being like the rest of us. His asceticism and generosity came at a price. Like the Latin American Bishops at the Council of Medellin, he made a preferential option for the poor, the mentally ill, the black and the gay. That was his choice and maybe some of us were jealous. I know I was! I'm not sure if Michael was familiar with these words of Archbishop Romero, but I think that they must have read the same Bible:

> I am a shepherd who, with his people, has begun to learn a beautiful and difficult truth: our Christian faith requires that we submerge ourselves in this world...

> The world that the Church must serve is the world of the poor and the poor are the ones who decide what it means to really live in the world. It is the poor who understand what is really taking place... the persecution of the church is the result of defending the poor. Our persecution is nothing less than sharing in the destiny of the poor. The poor are the body of Christ today. Through them, he lives on in history.

> From Oscar Romero's acceptance speech
> for an honorary doctorate at the Louvain.

Had Michael, like Oscar Romero, lived in San Salvador rather than Notting Hill, I doubt that he would have died in his bed, for prophets are a thorn in the side of the establishment. He too shared the fate of the poor of this country: to have his reputation attacked and to die a tedious, unglamorous death in an NHS hospital.

Not long before he died, Romero remarked, 'I have to confess that, as a Christian, I don't believe in death without resurrection. If they kill me, I will rise again in the Salvadoran people.' My guess is that Michael Hollings is alive and well in and among those he taught and served. I am minded of an Easter refrain I learned at L'Arche: *'Ne cherchez pas parmi les morts: il est resuscité!'* [Do not look among the dead: he is risen!]

Sheila Cassidy hit the headlines in 1975 when she was tortured and imprisoned for treating a wounded Revolutionary in Chile. She now works in Plymouth with cancer patients and has a special interest in young women with breast cancer and children who have lost a parent. She lectures widely, preaches occasionally and watches TV and sews in her spare time. She works as a Psychotherapist, writes books and is a passionate Arctophile.

CHAPTER SIX

Breaking down the Barriers: Parish Priest in Southall

MADELEINE SIMON

Michael Hollings arrived in Southall in September 1970 having done a considerable amount of homework regarding the area where he was about to become parish priest. This is evident from the letter he wrote to the Provincial Superior of the Society of the Sacred Heart about a group of sisters who hoped to start a small house in the town.

The Old Palace St Aldate's Oxford

1 July 1970

Dear Mother Eyre

Tremendous news that you are coming to Southall, i.e. setting up a small house there...

The need is exciting because it includes almost all the problems of megalopolis, Secular City, etc. I'll put some of them in order:

i. I think the largest single Indian population in the British Isles – very exclusive – basically not Christian. Desperate need to be among them and simply to be good and kind and pre-evangelical, living witness of our concern... when I was a stranger, etc.

ii. Catechetics – desperately short there.

iii. Parents – need to get at parents where they are – house visiting, catechetics – House Masses.

iv. Social work – a dearth in the parish – need to be concerned with families, marriage breakdowns, housing, unemployment, bad work conditions etc.

108

v.   Liturgy. Real lack of liturgical development and understanding. Practically no music. Lack of 'Family Mass'.

vi. Bad ecumenical relations. Baptists and Evangelicals opposing RCs joining council of churches. Methodists attacked for being friendly to RCs.

vii. St Anselm's School. English as a second language. Classes sometimes very heavily 'black'.

viii. Percentage in one area of the parish richer and more bourgeois – not keen to mix or mix in.

I am thrilled to go there and chose it as challenging for this day's world... Forgive my haste. God bless you.

Michael Hollings

For the previous eleven years Michael had been coming into contact mainly with undergraduates and their needs, with dons and with others around Oxford University. Liturgies had reflected the chaplaincy scene and there was little contact with the kind of life that Michael was to experience in Southall with its rich cultural mix. He would have had minimal contact with children of school and pre-school age and their parents. Nor had he experienced having six other committed people working full time with him: two assistant priests and four sisters. For that matter, neither had they experienced living alongside such a dynamic person as Michael Hollings.

He had undoubtedly a most attractive and winning personality, but he could be very demanding and sometimes seemed unaware that not everyone was capable of the total dedication that he demanded of himself. The situation was not without its problems, but overall the presbytery was a happy place for the priests and sisters concerned. They have contributed the following memories and reflections to this chapter.

At St Anselm's

THE PRIESTS

Fr Tony Brunning (Assistant Priest at St Anselm's, Southall, 1972-1978) writes:

'Living Priesthood was first published in 1977, the seventh of the eight years Michael Hollings spent in Southall. It was my privilege to share in six of those years. Michael did not just write about priesthood, he tried to live it. That's why his book is such a classic.

His letter, which preceded our first meeting, is a good illustration of his kindness and consideration for someone perhaps nervously contemplating a daunting appointment. I quote from it:

> Dear Tony, I hope this is not jumping any episcopal guns or causing confusion, but I am somewhat confused myself, so I thought I would write you a note.
>
> It is widely rumoured, and has some bishop backing, that you may be coming to join us here at St Anselm's. I've heard a bit about things which have and have not been happening to you, and I am very sorry that it has been so upsetting.
>
> Now I write tentatively, because I remain a little unsure if you have been asked to come here, if you want to come here and if you are coming here! What I'd like to say is 'Welcome', if you are. I can only say that I hope you will not find me too odd and difficult and unliveable-with, if you come. I think I can say that I have all sorts of nice ideas about teamwork, sharing responsibility, sharing ideas etc ...and then probably blast away at imposing my own petty ideas.

My first reaction was: 'What an amazing man' and so untypical of any parish priest I had met before. I am eternally grateful that I landed up in Southall for, without doubt, Michael Hollings has been the single most significant influence and inspiration in my continuing formation in 'Living Priesthood'.

When he was in the parish, Michael never had a day off. The nearest he came to that was when he went to Wakefield for a two-hour visit to a man seemingly with no family or friends, who was serving a life sentence in the prison there. He shrugged off my praise for this 'corporal work of mercy' by saying, 'Oh, it was wonderful – three hours in the comfort of British Rail without any disturbances from the phone or the front door – ideal for catching up on my correspondence!'

Michael may not have been the most patient of people, yet for all the irritations of open presbytery life, from the cat jumping on his desk and rearranging the manuscript for his latest book on prayer to a drunken burglar vomiting in the airing cupboard, the strongest word of condemnation that I ever heard him utter was 'tiresome'.

People of all varieties and conditions of life found a temporary home in the 'open house'. I remember when a community relations officer, who was actively engaged in parish life, was killed in a road accident on a foggy day in December. His wife had recently joined him from Nigeria with their six children aged between 3 and 14. She was deeply distressed, it was just before Christmas, and did not want to remain at home that night. At Michael's invitation they all bedded down in the presbytery.'

Fr Peter Sharp, who spent the years 1973–1976 in St Anselm's parish, adds his own experience of life as an assistant priest at that time:

'Coming from a traditional parish to St Anselm's Southall could not have been a greater culture shock. Nothing could have prepared me, except that I had been told to 'expect anything except the expected'.

During the day there were always parishioners in and out. For the most part the door was not locked. The large dining table was usually fully occupied at meal times and one never knew who would be present, which made for an interesting life, but with none of the privacy one had been used to.

The young men came in at various hours and in various moods according to how their day had gone. I remember one young Scot who marched up and down the landing until the early hours shouting curses against Roman Catholics. The same gentleman would often sit sideways at the table to avoid having any communication with us. The turning point came when several of us were separately angry with him for losing yet another job. He suddenly realised that we were people who cared about him – a wholly new experience, he later admitted.

Someone who knew Michael quite well warned me that, while he always had time for a person with a problem, he could sometimes get quite impatient when his time was taken up by someone else. Certainly Michael would come into his own when confronted with the most intractable of people or impossible situations. He seemed most happy to be on the fringe with all sorts of rejected and dejected individuals. His patience was sometimes short with us, but endless with those who tried him most.

Looking back at my time in Southall, it seemed we lived in a constant state of challenge and change. The local and cultural differences of the place, the racial riots and two stabbings of Indian youths created much of this, but it was Michael's response to the various problems which was often most challenging. Following a break-in, when Michael actually caught the intruder, I rushed downstairs and said that I would call the police. Michael had other ideas and put the kettle on to make everyone tea. The result was that we acquired another houseguest.'

Fr John Murphy was another who had the experience of living the priesthood in Michael's unique way. He recalls:

'A motif of Michael's ministry was the removal of barriers. Did he go too far? Was the 'open door' practice of the parish house good bridge building or dangerous dam breaching? One might think that the greater the outreach into the community and the greater the use of the house for meetings, all the greater would be the need for a secure home environment. The rules of a normal healthy day would support that view. This, however, was not the case and the parish house played host to some homeless older adolescents and young men, in some cases on probation.

The tensions which ferment in such a situation are usually resolved either by house rules or by descent into chaos and worse. The fact is that neither happened. Power and structures for sharing responsibility were not seen as the means to order life together, even when Michael was away. The house style was much more for Michael to confront the individual with his offending behaviour. As I once heard Michael shout at one of the lads, 'Don't you ever think of other people?', after which it was all over.

Such influence derives from strength of character based on a highly developed belief of the potential in people, coupled with a deep and practised love for each individual. It also needed confidence that each of the corrective moments were taken by the transgressor as learning ones, and so did not need backing up with a new rule to prevent such misconduct happening again. I can remember my car being 'borrowed' only once. As far as possible Michael dismantled barriers which restricted an individual's potential for taking charge of her or his own life.

There was, I believe, only one occasion when the priests of the house shared a meal alone. When I ask myself if I think that Michael's plan for open living – open door, no secrets, no power, minimal protection –went too far, I have to say that it felt like it. But if I ask myself whether there was any value in being stretched in self-confidence and responsibility by such leadership, I think I learnt that successful outcomes are not the hallmark of putting the gospel into practice. Most probably, the hallmark is knowing that God works through our shortcomings.'

THE SISTERS

When the Society of the Sacred Heart went to Southall, it was only a few years since Vatican II and the lifting of enclosure for the sisters. As well as having to deal with a larger-than-life priest, they were in the process of changing their dress from the habits they had been used to for the best part of thirty years, to normal civilian clothing. Added to all this, they were being asked to call the parish priest by his Christian name, something unheard of in their previous experience.

Michael was quick to perceive the situation and with great patience, some cajoling and some teasing, edged the sisters into their new role. He realised they had a lot to give to the realisation of his vision for the parish and he soon had them fully involved in the enterprises he was introducing. He quickly perceived the areas of commitment where each would be happiest. For example, he sensed the courage and creativity in Sister Josie, which was as yet largely latent. He asked her to visit a couple where he and others had failed to gain entrance. Undaunted, she went off to the address and discovered the reason for the unwillingness of the couple to allow anyone in. The husband had leprosy and was very disfigured. From then on Josie went regularly to visit them, bathing his sores as necessary.

THE PARISHIONERS

One of the first things Michael undertook after his arrival was to provide forms and pencils at every Mass on one particular Sunday for the parishioners to fill in who they were, where they lived and what they could offer by way of service to their parish. A few dedicated people undertook the considerable collation job with the presbytery team, and groups were then invited to the presbytery to discuss and put into action the service they had offered.

The survey covered the whole range of the areas listed in the letter at the beginning of this chapter, resulting in an almost military plan of action. Areas covered included organising weekday House Masses, the provision of catechetics for children not in St Anselm's School, the development of the already existing Union of Catholic Mothers, tackling problems of homelessness and of newly arrived and disorientated immigrants, and building relations with other churches and religions.

Michael's influence in the parish was manifold. Many people recall his kindness, his welcome and his self-giving, especially to the pastoral care of the sick. At St Anselm's, as at Oxford, his wider ministry of counselling and befriending drew many people closer to God and into the Church. Tibor Szende, now a monk at Quarr Abbey, remembers how Michael helped him during this time:

'I was a young student when I met Michael in 1970. He impressed me by his practical simplicity and his interest in other people's welfare. I had left my home in Hungary three years earlier and was losing direction in life. So I asked to speak to him and he listened to me. He was a good, empathic listener and I opened up and told him about my turbulent background and current disorientation, and asked if he had any advice to give. He said yes, and what he said was surprising, but almost meaningless to me: learn to love people and life will become much easier.

I had no idea what he was talking about but he offered me a pact: he would love me and I could learn to return his love. Once I had learned to love one person, he said, I could love anybody. I shrugged uncomprehendingly, but continued to visit him regularly. More and more he became like a father to me, always dependable, faithful and understanding, but not always patient. Over two decades I have come to understand what he meant by his love. It healed many wounds in me and helped me to grow out of my prolonged adolescence.

From the start I was overawed by his commitment to God. He talked about his personal relationship with God and it sounded just like a relationship between two people. I asked him if God was available in this way for just a selected few, but he assured me that he was there for anybody who wanted him. I went and sat beside him in church during his early morning hour of prayer, neither feeling nor seeing anything, just hanging in there in the hope that he was right and that something would happen to me too. In the years to come it did happen and now I too have a personal relationship with God.

I owed Michael much and I pray for him, although I think that the Lord welcomed him with the words, "Come, O blessed of my Father, inherit the kingdom prepared for you from the foundation of the world."'

ECUMENICAL AND NON-CHRISTIAN RELATIONS

When Michael arrived in Southall in 1970, there were five Anglican churches, a Baptist church, and the Methodist King's Hall. There were also three Hindu temples, two gurdwaras (Sikh places of worship) and two mosques. Michael personally made friends with the leaders of all these places of worship, Christian and non-Christian alike.

An ecumenical fraternal, already existing, was expanded at his request to include the Methodist deaconess, an Anglican woman lay worker and one of the Catholic sisters. The monthly meeting did much to further good relations among the Christian denominations. During one of these meetings, however, there was an awkward moment when, at the final period of prayer, someone made an intervention calling on God to forgive the Church of England for negotiating the sale to the Hindu community of an Anglican church which had become redundant. In his view they were handing over a consecrated building to Satan. There was an appalled silence all round and then Michael said very quietly, 'I cannot say Amen to that prayer.' Integrity was satisfied without confrontation.

It was during the 1970s that young members of the National Front took it upon themselves to persecute the Asian and Afro-Caribbean young people of Southall. This culminated in the murder of a teenage Sikh on the steps of the Dominion Cinema next to St Anselm's Church. Michael immediately invited the leaders of all denominations and religions to meet with him to discuss what could be done to lower the temperature in the town, and between them they came up with the idea of holding a peace march. The planning responsibilities were shared out to the effect that all, Christians and non-Christians alike, worked together. The route had to be organised, and the Civic Centre and Police brought on board.

117

Placards were thought out and made, with slogans such as 'One Race – the Human Race' and 'We Want Peace'. The event was widely advertised.

A great number of Southall people turned out and so too did a gang of disaffected youths who arrived by train from central London (and whom the police called the Rent-a-Mob because they appeared at every protest march available). But the police were prepared and shepherded them to the back of the procession from where they proceeded to shout slogans of their own, such as ones supporting Enoch Powell. The march was led by the Anglican bishop of the area and the religious leaders of Southall. The marching was in silence except for a group of West Indian women standing at a road junction, singing 'We shall overcome'. The Television News

that evening showed only the shouting Rent-a-Mob group which gave the impression that the whole event was confrontational and chaotic. In fact, it had ended in a small park where everyone had sat on the grass to listen to a man from the Civic Centre speaking about peace. At the end he called for a show of hands for peace and the whole field rose to the challenge. A small group from St Anselm's Church went to the TV company's offices to complain of the unfair and misleading coverage. They were shown the uncut film and it was agreed that the part covering the show of hands for peace across the park would be shown. It was, albeit at 11.30pm.

Michael with Mother Teresa at St Anselm's

Towards the end of his time in Southall, Michael made contact with

Mother Teresa and invited her Missionaries of Charity into the parish. This was their first community in Britain, and second in Europe, after Rome.

Shortly before he left Southall in 1978, the Sikh community of the town invited him to meet them to thank him for his friendship and positive attitude towards the various nationalities and cultures in the town. They made him an honorary Sikh and presented him with a turban and the right to wear it. Michael was very touched by this gesture.

His whole eight years in Southall proved to be a good preparation for his work at St Mary of the Angels.

Sister Madeleine Simon is a Religious of the Sacred Heart (RSCJ). After many years of teaching young children she became a Lecturer in Education at Digby Stuart College of Education. She lived at Southall for eleven years.

CHAPTER SEVEN

Open Door

PAUL MILANOWSKI

The open doors of the church and the parish house at St Mary of the Angels on the edge of Notting Hill, were Fr Michael Hollings' singular signature. They were also the symbol of the openness of his inner city and priestly ministry.

Spring, summer, autumn and winter, the doors were literally left wide open, inviting everyone to walk in. Women and men of the road, parishioners, residents of the house, all came and went through the same open doors. Living there, one got used to anyone and everyone, including the Duke and Duchess of Norfolk, Dr Sheila Cassidy, Etta Gullick, Cardinal Hume, Mother Teresa of Calcutta, authors, artists, actors, musicians, doctors, nurses and lawyers, professors, missionaries and theologians, friends and acquaintances, priests and religious, all climbing the winding stairs and walking the corridors looking for Fr Michael, some member of the team or house, or a cup of tea.

Many people, out of curiosity, would enter the church or simply look in. Many would enter the parish house just because the doors were open. (Incidentally, Michael never the used the word presbytery or rectory. He wanted the place to be known as the Parish House, signifying that it was a house for the parish and not just for the priests.) One might have to walk through a cluster of people sitting on the steps waiting for sandwiches, or occasionally have to climb over someone, or their belongings, blocking the way. In the seven years I lived there, I can remember only a few instances of theft, destruction, or physical violence, and that in a neighbourhood notorious for crime, drugs, inner city poverty and homelessness.

Padre Pio in 1947, the year Michael first met him.

Fr. Jock Dalrymple, senior, and his nephew Jock, in January 1985, 8 months before the former's death.

Pictures taken at the Notting Hill carnival.

Pictures taken at the Notting Hill carnival.

Michael at his desk

'Michael's room' – at St Mary of the Angels.
Painted by Tarka Kings.

The open doors were only part of living in an open house, as espoused and envisioned by Michael. The parish house and church doors were open from 8.30 am until 7.30pm, seven days a week. It was a house of great hospitality, but not in the Catholic Worker sense. Michael's persistent aim was to create a community of all sorts of people. In three separate buildings we all lived under the single roof of Michael's invitation.

Michael clearly and selectively tried to have the house mirror the inner city neighbourhood. Residents included priests, deacons, seminarians and religious, men and women, young and old, black and white, rich and poor, Christian and non-Christian, married and single, straight and gay, widowed and divorced, professionals, employed, unemployed, community service volunteers, and recently released prison inmates. That was the open house.

Living there was a bit like living with Captain Noah in the Ark, as one of the curates famously wrote in one of the Sunday newsletters. It was never easy; never fully successful. Sharing the same table, meeting and praying together, discussing the Sunday Scripture readings over soup on Mondays, making and serving sandwiches and tea and taking on some of the household chores and parish responsibilities, was a constant challenge. It could be a struggle for Michael to achieve harmony and co-operation from all the residents.

In his book *Living Priesthood*, Michael writes: 'The inspiration of Vatican II was to open windows, let in fresh air and so, following the same analogy, to raise a certain amount of dust.' Many people consider the open door policy to be heroic and contagious. Others felt it to be foolish and dangerous. There could be 'aggro' and agony, heated debates, misunderstanding, conflict and vituperation. At times there were angry neighbours and concerned parishioners. Despite it all, Michael was resolute. He maintained an open house in Oxford, Southall and St Mary of the Angels. It cost him dear, personally, and probably contributed to his diabetes and mood swings; it also left him vulnerable to tabloid accusation in the very last years of his ministry and life.

Race and religion were inseparable for Michael. In the parish, the parish school, the parish house, in his own personal life, and in the community, he fought the sin and scandal of racism with every weapon at his disposal. He endeavoured to bring down the walls of separation and segregation by bringing people of various races, religions and lifestyles together in prayer, in service, in community projects and in the shared life of the parish house.

The highlight of the year for Michael and his inner city ministry at St Mary of the Angels was the Notting Hill Carnival, beginning with the parish Carnival Mass (during the August Bank Holiday weekend). Over the years he enthusiastically supported and endorsed the grandest carnival celebration in Europe.

For Michael the Notting Hill Carnival was a powerful vehicle of building race relations and breaking down prejudice and racism. The Carnival had this effect through encouraging ethnic pride, music, pageantry, parade, spectacle, colourful costumes, dance, street parties and celebrations, and ethnic foods. Preparation for Carnival began the week after the previous Carnival, with meetings deciding a biblical or theological theme for the parish. This theme would be applied to the parish children's band and the Carnival Mass. Often, meetings with police and Westminster City Council authorities were held to discuss and resolve problems and difficulties, as well as to provide an opportunity to confront covert and overt racism both at Carnival and in the community throughout the year.

Equal in effort and enthusiasm to the Carnival, for Michael, were the Christmas Dinners and parties held every year. Dinner on Christmas Day was for the elderly, Boxing Day was a thank you for all who worked and helped in the parish, the day after that was for men and women of the road. In reality it was not unusual to find a number of individuals at all three dinners!

With military discipline, Michael planned the menu, prepared all the soup, roasted, carved and served the turkeys, while a long line of recruits complemented his efforts with stuffing, potatoes, gravy, vegetables, bread and beverages. Michael the master chef and *maitre d'* was a harsh taskmaster. He wanted his visitors to feel relaxed and waited upon as welcome guests; they must not be rushed or feel part of some anonymous process. Accordingly, if some well-meaning helper began collecting dinner plates before all were finished, Michael would bellow at the top of his voice, 'Not yet, my dear!' He remained at his post cooking, serving and cleaning up, until the very end, long after many of his recruits had gone home.

Michael was a people priest. From the first day of his ordination he was determined to be part of the community he served. He rejected a priesthood and clerical life that was in any way detached from the people. With boundless energy, Michael spent endless hours with people in his room, in the parish house, at schools, on many governing boards, in the neighbourhood and community, in lectures, talks, retreats, on pilgrimages, on the phone, and through his writing and voluminous correspondence.

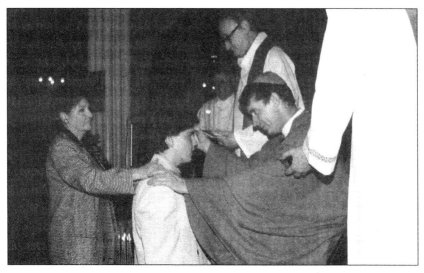

Confirmation at St Mary of the Angels with Bishop John Crowley

The heart of his ministry and priesthood was the eucharist. He loved cele- brating Mass with the faithful. He lived the Eucharist as the summit, source and centre of all Christian prayer and worship. Parish and home liturgies, early morning convent Masses, Notting Hill Carnival Masses, celebrating for prisoners and the handicapped, even simply bedside Masses for the sick: these were all a vital ingredient of Michael's ministry.

The inner city gave him endless opportunities to celebrate the Eucharist with a great diversity of groups and individuals. After Michael's Funeral Mass at Westminster Cathedral, a man came into St Mary of the Angels to pray and pay his respects to Michael. Inside the porch there was a Book of Consolation in which people had been invited to write. He read it with growing anguish on his face, distressed to discover that Michael had died and that he had missed the service. He said, 'You know, this lovely priest used to say Mass with us street traders in Portobello Road once a year in memory of all them who had died.'

Michael embraced everyone – literally. His inner city ministry embraced the homeless, the poor, pensioners and racial minorities. The open doors of the parish house, the church and his own room were literally and symboli- cally open to all. From morning to night the open door invited and wel- comed everyone, including the great number of mentally and emotionally disturbed people who lived in the area. Ideally the door was open to find Jesus the Good News, prayer, peace, a friend, a cup of tea and hospitality.

Two unlikely soul companions in his open door inner city ministry were the Carmelite nun, St Thérèse of Lisieux, and the Franciscan Friar, Padre Pio. From these two companions Michael surely found models for min- istry in the inner city of London, examples for him of personal vulnera- bility and the strength of prayer.

Michael inherited devotion to St Thérèse – the Little Flower – from his mother. It was a veneration that was personal, with Thérèse's little way of prayer, her devotion to the eucharist, her dedication to the missions, and her desire 'to please God in all things', as well as her simple guidance in love and suffering. Michael referred to Thérèse in talks and articles, and even wrote a book about her life. She helped him in the complexities of inner city existence to live a simple life himself and to remain focussed on the essentials of ministry.

Stigmatic Padre Pio touched Michael when he was studying at the Beda in Rome. Michael was deeply moved by Padre Pio's 'obedience', his prayer, and his personal contact with the sick and the poor. All these were constants and fundamentals in Michael's inner city ministry of openness to all.

Michael's last year of life and ministry was also marked by the stigmata – the crucifixion wounds of Jesus. The wounds were of a painful spiritual and psychological kind. Following a newspaper allegation, Michael was stigmatised by public accusation,. As is now routine in such matters, he was suspended from the parish and all pastoral ministry. Indeed, he was forced to remove himself from the people he loved and

Sr Carmel, Rosa Guerra and Joan Cooley.

served. This was followed by months of suffering in silence and obedience, prayer and loneliness, in a state of rapid physical decline. After investigation by the authorities he was restored as parish priest of St Mary of the Angels, to the acclamation of his people, but he did not have long to live.

The final words should be his own, from the Afterword to *Living Priesthood*:

> For me, the 'witness' of an open house is one witness of the Incarnation of Jesus Christ. He was available, sometimes he had nowhere to lay his head, he was surrounded and pressed on all sides. He was happy to be with sinners. However ineffective this living may be, no matter. What matters is that it is there. Pray God that all the marvellous developments in the Church, plans, rites etc will not totally remove the gospel from the poor. There is grave danger here. Mere talk of poverty and the poor is worthless. If you are a lay person, a student for the priesthood, a priest or higher rank – make an option for the poor however difficult it is to live it out. Prayer is the foundation, love is the energiser, humility is the way in Christ.
>
> *Michael Hollings*

Paul Milanowski is a priest of the diocese of Grand Rapids, Michigan, where he is currently vocations promoter among college students following many years of parish ministry. In the spring of 1985 he was deeply dismayed by the evidence of US involvement in wars in the Central American countries of Guatemala, Nicaragua and El Salvador. In his own words, 'This led me to a kind of resistance by leaving and not paying taxes.' With the permission of his bishop he came to Britain, where he lived and worked as a member of the parish team at St Mary of the Angels until the summer of 1992.

CHAPTER EIGHT

Ecumenist and Catholic

TERRY TASTARD

You walked down Westbourne Grove, where Chinese, Indian and Arab shops offered a profusion of exotic foods to London passers-by. A turn or two brought you to Moorhouse Road, a street of fading gentility on the edge of Notting Hill. Here the parish house of St Mary of the Angels sat with a baronial brick front. Indeed, the mock medieval front door, complete with grill, might have seemed forbidding, were it not for the fact that the door was almost always propped open.

Once inside you walked up a broad sweep of steps, where you might find a few men of the road waiting for tea and sandwiches. You passed the spot where the huge wall mirror had stood until it was wrenched off and spirited into a taxi by thieves. (Rumour had it that the mirror was spotted on an antiques stall in nearby Portobello Road.) Through the swing doors you went, up a spiral staircase of bright red steps. The staircase wound its way up inside a neogothic turret. On the first floor you entered a scruffy little corridor. On the notice board on the left you would find a thin sheet of paper with Michael's engagements for the day written down for everyone to see. Counselling, committees, funerals, Mass, visits to the sick: all were jotted down, each with its stipulated time. You would check to see that your name was there, then sneak a look at who else Michael was seeing that day.

From the windowless kitchen out of sight to the right, you would hear the sounds of Maureen or Doris creating a meal from the date-expired food given by the shops. You turned left down the corridor to Michael's room, where the door would be open and Michael himself would be bent over

127

the desk, writing a letter while the tiny portable radio blathered away next to him. The creak of the floorboard outside the door would give you away and Michael would look up at you, smiling. He always seemed unaccountably pleased to see you.

I trod this path many times, first to Michael as a friend, then to him as the priest preparing me for reception into full communion with the Catholic Church. Then I lived in the house for a year. Even after leaving, my steps returned many times as I sought Michael's counsel and the sacrament of reconciliation. Many other people found their way to his room in Moorhouse Road, as part of finding their way into the Catholic Church. Similarly in Westminster Cathedral, Oxford University and Southall, Michael's open ear and open heart had helped many people find God and to enter the fullness of Catholic faith. Yet here is what on the surface at least appears a conundrum: this same man was full of respect for other Christian traditions. Genuine respect, often mixed with affection and admiration. For him, Christians in other churches were brothers and sisters, and their work and witness a means of grace. They made Jesus Christ known and loved, and he felt that in this he shared a ministry with them.

How could Michael both be such a vibrant Catholic, and yet so ecumenically appreciative? Perhaps I could explore this apparent tension – an example to us all – by relating something of my own story. I first met Michael Hollings in March 1979, at which time I was an Anglican Franciscan friar. I was part of a small group of brothers who met at St Mary of the Angels to discuss whether we should open a house in the area. He left us to make up our own minds, but gave discreet encouragement when we decided to go ahead. Later that year I was part of the Franciscan group that established Holy Trinity House in Paddington. Our coordinator was Brother Thaddaeus SSF, who had previously run an extended community in the Harrow Road area for three or four years, welcoming homeless into the house and supporting himself by taking menial jobs. Holy Trinity House envisioned continuing this ministry, but on a bigger scale. With Thaddaeus' experience and Michael's example down the road, we were soon up and running.

Looking back from the late 1990s, it is hard to recapture now the mixture of anger and near despair felt by concerned Christians in the early 1980s. The Thatcher government seemed determined to sweep away much of the support system that had kept the poor and homeless from sinking. Vast sums were spent on nuclear arms. Unemployment and homelessness exploded at a frightening rate. Like St Mary of the Angels, Holy Trinity House was in the City of Westminster. All around us we could see Westminster council homes boarded up with heavy steel shutters, until they could be sold. At the same time, local boarding houses were bursting with families who were sent to emergency accommodation in these 'Bed and Breakfasts' while council homes were kept empty around them.

Our Franciscan community combined caring ministry with justice and peace involvement on a wider scale. There was always a small number of people living with us who were finding a path to healing from addictions, or other personal difficulties. We also joined local and national groups involved in such issues as homelessness, disarmament and the Third World. Two Franciscan sisters were also part of our community: one was a leader in the women's movement, another was a nurse in a day centre for the homeless. I tried to combine academic work with social justice work, although in the long run it was an impossible mixture to sustain. This combination of ministries might have seemed an unusual commitment for a Franciscan community. On the other hand, the chapel was the first room that we set up in the house. We prayed the offices there and celebrated the Eucharist daily. On Sunday evenings we had a quiet hour of exposition of the Blessed Sacrament.

In some ways our life resembled aspects of life in St Mary of the Angels down the road. Occasionally Michael himself would come in to visit, and sometimes date-expired food made its way up the road to help us out. I found myself increasingly drawn to St Mary of the Angels. What drew me was partly his personality, but I was also drawn by the feel of the worship in the church. The church building itself was a neogothic gem with a slight edge of chaos. Electric cables were draped on walls. There was an indifferent altar with plastic candle holders. Posters showed children's work or CAFOD campaigns. (Michael was never strong on aesthetics.) On the other hand, the church seemed to combine homeliness and mystery. Like home, you felt at ease. You even accepted the occasional disruptions caused by the mentally unstable – for did not every family have its odder elements? There was a depth of silence and a prayerfulness which drew you deeper into meditation and intercession. At Sunday Mass there was again a strong sense of family, and a wonderful kaleidoscope of races and nationalities. When Michael celebrated Mass, he did so in a direct, uncomplicated manner. Perhaps his style was even rather clipped and might have reflected his military years. But he always managed to convey that this was what life and faith were all about. Watch him at Mass and you knew that he believed. Similarly, in his preaching, he spoke directly and simply about Jesus, and encouraged us to love and serve and pray and if necessary suffer like Jesus.

I noticed that while Michael had a strong commitment to social justice, he avoided the grand gesture. He was not partisan. In his view, people of good will and sincerity of heart were to be found mucking in, wanting to do something to help. It was this, rather than the purity of their political thought, that mattered to him. He managed to be firm friends with people on both left and right of the political spectrum. Not that Michael lacked commitment: he served long hours on the committee of a local organization working with the young unemployed, for example. He also worked hard to overcome racism. He went out into the streets to help cool tensions when in earlier years the Notting Hill Carnival threatened to spin out of control in confrontations between police and local black youths. But in ethnic affairs he preferred the positive example. Each year the parish's contribution to the Carnival was outstanding, with its own float, the school children costumed, and above all the explosive, joyful, Carnival Mass.

This Mass was one living example of his commitment to Christian unity, for people from all traditions in the community crammed into the church for this roof-lifting occasion. It was a symbol of his constant desire that Christians should not only speak words of unity but somehow find ways of living them, of celebrating what they had in common in Christ. In Oxford he worked closely with the Anglican college chaplains, for example in organising a summer camp where Oxford students could welcome lads from Borstals. In Southall he was delighted when it became necessary, for various reasons, to hold one of the Sunday Masses in a local Anglican church. In Moorhouse Road his church was literally on the boundary of Notting Hill and Paddington. No problem: for Michael this was an opportunity to meet regularly with clergy and community leaders from two areas, to pray with them, to eat with them, to ponder with them the challenge of ministry in the inner city. When High Anglicans asked him to write a book which would help them to renewal, he wrote *Hearts not Garments* (1982) where he showed real understanding of the Anglican position and quoted from Anglican writers like Bede Frost. Later, Michael was a keynote speaker at their conference, where, typically, he warned them against triumphalism. His words near the beginning of the book are, however, addressed to Christians of all traditions: 'In the whole Church of Christ, which has been so often and so painfully rent with dissension and even bloody fratricide, we need to share everything in Christ and in the Church, so that we do indeed build up in love.'

Bit by bit I found myself gravitating towards his parish. It offered one way of seeing lively Catholicism (I knew even then that there could be many other ways). In fact, for 20 years I had been fighting the desire to become a Catholic. One of my bizarre memories is going into the Catholic Cathedral in Johannesburg, feeling myself drawn to becoming a Catholic, and praying that I might remain a faithful Anglican! Michael must have sensed my growing appreciation of Catholic life and spirituality. Yet he never fished. He was always respectful and supportive of our own calling as Anglican Franciscans. His only criticism came when he felt that worldly comfort was creeping into our community life. How could he be so respectful on the one hand and yet so magnetic on the other? So strong for ecumenism and yet able to draw others into the Catholic faith?

I think the explanation is that Michael believed in the mystery of God's activity in each person. As a priest, as a spiritual director, as a counsellor, he believed that no one was untouched by God. Part of his job was to help people be responsive to God's grace, to see where and how God was at work in their lives. We need to remember that contemporary English usage has somewhat distorted the idea of mystery. It has come to mean obscurity, bafflement, as in the expression, 'It's all a mystery to me.' But the religious roots of mystery are rather different. Mystery is that which we can discern or partially grasp, but will never fully control or completely comprehend. My favourite image of mystery is that of a spring bubbling away. You can see it, hear it, taste the water and be refreshed by it, but you can never get to its source, which leads back through time to the rain of centuries trickling down. The divine life in humans is a mystery in the sense that we can sometimes feel it in us, or see its power in others and, if we are alert, we can see it heal and change and challenge, but its ultimate source is always beyond our grasp.

Michael believed in this presence and power of God in the lives of people. Because he knew it came from God, he was respectful of what the Spirit was doing and where it was moving. In turn, he was respectful of people's response to God's work in them. It was enough for him if through their faith they loved more, served more, prayed more. That was a sign that God was at work in them. He knew that Catholics had no monopoly of Christian love and service. He would say more than this. In fact, he would say that he had learned from other Christians. In *Living Priesthood* he writes: 'Personally speaking, the experience of sharing has been vitalising. It is easy to stay inside one's tradition and to grow narrower. The insights and traditions of others have constantly reminded me of the vast range of truth and goodness, which is too big to be grasped equally effectively all the time.' Here we see his acceptance of God as revelation but also of God as mystery. Michael, then, found the life of

God within the Catholic Church but also beyond it. Similarly, he recognised the work of the Spirit if people found courage to seek healing from addictions or to tackle distressing circumstances through repentance. God was this mysterious presence. This living mystery was known through his effects, but was always a step ahead of us and infinitely greater than our greatest understanding. Michael bowed before the mystery. Hence people of many faiths could feel comfortable with Michael.

At the same time, Michael knew that for some people the power and presence of God was drawing them into the Catholic Church. He understood well that for some who were already Christian, a fuller, more sacramental faith was what would best build them up and nourish them. He never sought to persuade people to change their allegiance, but if they felt the divine mystery in them attracting them to the Catholic Church, then he would be supportive: encouraging them, but always challenging them to take God seriously, whatever their tradition. Because he himself was so rooted and nourished in the Catholic faith, it was inevitable that people who were drawn to Catholicism would seek him out. They would want something of what they discerned in him: a Catholic faith which enabled a deeper love of God and neighbour.

One summer's day in 1987, I went out for lunch with him. I mentioned that I had been struggling for years not to become a Catholic. He replied simply that if I felt God calling me into the Catholic Church then I should take it seriously. I was not ready to hear this. As soon as he said that, I felt beset by panic. Where would I go? What would I do? Much of my identity seemed to revolve around being an Anglican Franciscan friar. I drew back in fright. I cannot recall making any substantial reply to Michael. We met many times after that, and he never referred to what I had said on that occasion. As part of his respect for the divine mystery, he waited to see what God would do and how I would respond to God.

By June 1989 a series of events had brought me through a period of profound heart-searching and anxiety to a decision which I dreaded. I had to leave the Anglican Church, become a Catholic and hope that some day the Catholic Church might allow me to test my vocation to the priesthood. Again I went out for lunch with Michael and told him of my decision. I also told him of my deep fears, of my anguish at leaving so much behind, at my shame of not respecting the lifelong commitment I had made to the Franciscans. He was enormously reassuring. So often, at such times, people found in Michael a calm, steadying love that would slow them down and help them concentrate on the next move. Michael showed you that 'one step enough' could help you make a long journey, a stage at a time. No point getting bewildered about the miles far ahead. Rather, seek the next step. At the time, the parish house was full, but he promised to find a place for me as soon as possible. This was very important: all I had was a temporary home with a friend, and little money. He encouraged me to believe in God's presence in our world. Michael said to me once, 'I believe that God's about, and I try myself to be out and about and see what God is doing.' He felt that the more I could believe in God's work in the world and in my life, the calmer I would be and the next step would become clear, and the step after that. He was right. I found a job with a movement for faith and justice, and he soon found a place for me at St Mary of the Angels. I moved into that cheerful, chaotic household for a year.

Michael prepared me for reception into the Catholic Church. I suppose that some might feel that I should have come through the RCIA route, but he accepted that I had a good basic knowledge of the Christian faith and indeed of Catholic teaching. Even so, he did not rush me. He gave me time to identify stumbling blocks, time to ponder his answers. Occasionally over the years I have heard it said or implied that Michael was a hopeless liberal. Those who think this, should think again. Michael would not let me move on until I had come to a full understanding and acceptance of the Catholic faith. There was no evading the difficult areas. We looked at them, as well as at other aspects of Catholic teaching, and he waited for my head to catch up with my heart and for my acceptance of what the Church taught.

Beyond the church teaching itself, however, there lay always the mystery of God. Michael wanted people to believe, but he also wanted people to be in touch with God and to know the love of God shown in the face of Jesus Christ. Michael himself knew the mystery in the sense of having been opened up to its depths. For him, faith was summed up in St John's words: 'God is love.' God's power was his love, and God's knowledge was his love. God's self revelation was on the Cross – an act of love in history that would stand for ever. If you went to Michael for guidance, confession, or encouragement, you felt loved, and the love flowed from his own openness to God. You also felt taken seriously, perhaps more seriously than you took yourself. Michael would not allow you to evade the question: Is God in your life? And if so, how are you responding?

He himself was on a journey. He helped many people into the Church and yet he himself sought conversion in the sense of *metanoia*, the ongoing shaping of heart and spirit in accordance with the mind of Christ. As such he struggled with himself like everybody else. For example, he could have an appalling temper, and go off like a rocket, although he was usually the first to apologise. Tiredness got the better of him sometimes, especially as the years went by. Above all, there was a frustrating mixture in him: part of him wanted to let go and genuinely delegate to others, while another part of him kept on wanting to assert control. Above all, he pushed himself too hard, and tried to ignore his crumbling body. In this respect, Michael reminded me of St Francis of Assisi, who apologised on his deathbed to 'Brother Ass', his body, for all the burdens he had inflicted on it over the years. Michael knew that he had failings, but as he grew older he mellowed towards himself, extending to himself something of the compassion he had always extended to others.

He had found Christ, or rather been found by Christ, but he knew that the journey would not be over until the light of the resurrection dawned on him. Like – dare I say it? – a good Quaker, Michael saluted that which is of God in every person. But like a good Catholic, he loved the road he trod, the way of the saints and the sacraments where so many had travelled before him. Something of this love rubbed off on to others, and they wanted to walk this road with him. If you wanted him to do so, he would show you the road. He was the convert's friend, but like the best of mentors he knew when to let go in order to send you on your way with his blessing.

Terry Tastard is a priest of the Diocese of Westminster. The author of a book on spirituality and social justice, he has also contributed to other books and journals. In addition to parish ministry he is currently researching Christian responses to the Holocaust as part of a postgraduate research programme at the University of Hertfordshire.

CHAPTER NINE

Spreading the Word
JOAN MCCRIMMON

Books can tell us quite a lot about prayer but they cannot teach us how to pray. The best they can do is stir us up to want to pray and help us recognise the process of discovery and practice. We are more truly helped by someone who is experienced in the art of praying. The human voice, the look of sympathy and understanding, the back and forth of conversation, give us, at least in the early stages, the confidence to try to pray.

'Master, teach us to pray as John taught his disciples.' Michael Hollings followed this direct approach with a very human touch, so much so that his talks to students at Oxford were passed around the University on scraps of paper, which were eventually carefully gathered and, after pressure from the students, passed on to us to publish. However, *Day by Day* was not the first book by Michael published by our company, nor indeed was it his first published work.

During the late sixties and early seventies great changes were happening in many Catholic parishes. Mayhew-McCrimmon, the company I had founded with Kevin Mayhew, was heavily involved in producing new hymns from many different sources, to meet the needs of the revised liturgy. The gentle folk style of new composers such Estelle White, Miriam Therese Winter and the late Sebastian Temple, seemed to speak to people and encourage them to take an active part in the new form of Mass which had recently been introduced. Kevin Mayhew, himself a composer who had trained at the Westminster Choir School under George Malcolm, had recognised this great need for a simple direct approach to liturgical music in parishes. In our first hymnbooks, these new, more informal songs were intermingled with the best loved traditional hymns, together forming a mix-

137

ture of old and new which reached out to parishes everywhere, with amazing popularity, until such time as the liturgy in the vernacular settled down.

As well as running a publishing house, we organised a church choir that was often invited to share this new music with other parishes. A record was produced and the choir was frequently invited to broadcast and appear in religious programmes on television. In 1971 we were asked by the BBC to provide a sequence of three half-hour Sunday morning slots but including prayer as well as music. I scoured the Christian bookshops in London for material that would be sympathetic to our chosen songs – without much success. Eventually we chose excerpts from *Prayers of Life* by Michel Quoist.

"Why don't we publish our own Prayer books?" I asked Kevin, at one of our production meetings. He immediately picked up the telephone and rang Michael Hollings. "Joan wants some prayers that will talk to people – simple and direct – can you help?" So started the publishing relationship with Michael Hollings that was to last until his death in 1997.

Etta Gullick

Michael had written two popular books about the Christian life, *Hey, You!* and *Purple Times*, in the mid 1950's, published by Burns and Oates, but he had never written or assembled a book of prayers. He enlisted an Anglican colleague of his at Oxford, Etta Gullick, to help him. Etta was a theology lecturer at St Stephen's House – and had attracted a student following, keen to 'pray betta with Etta!' Her talent for research and keeping everything in order was to be invaluable in the preparation of the many books they wrote together.

138

We could not have dreamt how popular these prayer collections would become. The first, *The One Who Listens* was in its third printing within a month of publication and is still in demand over twenty-five years later. *It's Me O Lord* quickly followed and achieved even greater sales!

The two books were very different. *The One Who Listens* gathers together prayers for 'moods, crises, joys, sufferings and all life's events', including prayers for 'thanksgiving, joy and praise', 'forgiveness and opening up' and 'darkness and unbelief'. Michael and Etta drew on such diverse figures as John of the Cross, Thomas More, Kierkegaard, Newman, Quoist, Mother Teresa and many others. Two contrasting excerpts illustrate the wide ranging tone of the collection. A prayer of C. S. Lewis, an Oxford don, is followed by one by Bill, an undergraduate.

> From all my lame defeats and oh! much more
> From all the victories that I seemed to score;
> From cleverness shot forth on my behalf,
> At which, while angels weep, the audience laugh;
> From all my proofs of thy divinity
> Thou, who wouldst give no sign, deliver me.

> It is a relief to realise that you know exactly how I feel,
> what I can say honestly, and what I wish I could say,
> but can't just now. So on this basis I am able to finish
> quite honestly by saying
>
> with love
>
> from
>
> Bill.

It's Me O Lord on the other hand was a collection of Michael and Etta's own prayers. Their collection of informal prayers growing out of people's daily concerns managed in a simple and straightforward way to communicate the idea of prayer. 'The whole of life', as the authors wrote in their introduction, 'can be lived with God. It is the most natural thing in the world to cry out to God during the day for different reasons. Prayers can be made in many words, in short silences, in a single word, a glance, a sigh. Prayers may be superficial, made on a surface level, or so deep as to involve our whole being.'

During the first year of publication *The One Who Listens* sold over 40,000 copies and *It's Me O Lord* topped 50,000 in the same period. These prayer books, like the music collections, seemed to have touched a nerve in responding to the needs of the time. They were experienced as a breath of fresh air in a market place which was searching for something that would help people to respond to the demands of Vatican II with all its swift, baffling, exciting, and often painful changes. I have scanned the Company's scrapbook of reviews hoping to discover additional reasons for the immense popularity of these first two books. They make fascinating reading.

The Universe described Michael 'as at the forefront of implementers of the reforming decisions of the Second Vatican Council', while Douglas Brown, a religious broadcaster speaking on Radio 4, thought *The One Who Listens* had been 'compiled with such sensitivity and spirituality I'm inclined to say it will become a classic of its kind for our time'. *The Tablet* agreed, asserting that the anthology was 'of such variety that no individual stifled for expression could fail somewhere or other in these pages to find his inmost inchoate searching given an utterance', which was 'a major achievement'. It went on to describe how at the launch in the precincts of Westminster Abbey, the Dean welcomed the bringing together of joint concerns and joined prayers, commenting "this is an occasion where there are no barriers – Christians are at long last finding their long lost unity."

The Church Times was equally positive about *It's Me, O Lord*: 'the introduction... makes the essential point about prayer – that it may take any number of forms, any and all which are right so long as it brings me to God as I really am. Again the prayers themselves illustrate how this may be done in a great variety of human situations – by no means all miserable! There are many everyday subjects.' *The Catholic Herald* was also very enthusiastic. 'The tone of the prayers is informal, spontaneous and simple, some are for occasions of the most trivial kind – such as patience under the trials of in-laws! But the book has a truly Christian approach to life and to the very human condition of weakness and yet longing for the infinite. Even if you prefer to pray in your own words, read these prayers; the authors have a rare understanding of what Christianity is all about.'

In the same year, 1972, we published *Day by Day*. Patrick Keane in the *Catholic Gazette* described it as 'a refreshing and humble presentation of a way to God from one who has experienced in his own life the darkness of unbelief before achieving his present personal relationship with God, a relationship that could well be envied. The book will be welcomed by those probing for God and uninitiated in the art of prayer. It does not dwell on "how" to pray, but rather on being guided along a gentle path of development in prayer life.'

Michael not only encouraged people to pray in his books, he also encouraged others to write their own collections which in turn he asked us to publish!

Sheila Hurst, for example, was diagnosed with incurable cancer and was given a year to live in 1975. Michael at that time was parish priest at St Anselm's in Southall, often visiting Sheila and encouraging her to put her prayer thoughts on paper. As Sheila wrote in her book, *Shaken by the Wind*, 'Michael gave me the courage to write an autobiography of conversations I had with God.' The wind of the title was the Holy Spirit who was her constant source of strength – and which kept her going well beyond that one year…

Another writer whose first manuscript reached our publishing house via Michael was Rosa George, who wrote six pocket books of prayer – for

Women, Everyday, Anytime, Now, Today and *Love*. Rosa made moments into sacraments and not only wrote prayers for times like morning, the seasons and growing old, but also for moments that could otherwise pass away in idleness. She talked to God in a lovely way, which we can share through her writing.

> Beloved Jesus
> help me
> not to pass by
> for fear of becoming
> too involved,
> but in your caring wisdom
> to open wide my arms
> in order that
> we might hold each other
> and learn from each other
> in your love.

A Pocket Book of Prayers for Today

Rosa's books became so popular that during the 1980's she was voted Catholic Woman of the Year. She had encountered many problems in her life, and her writing not only helped her through the bad times but continues to help many others.

Among Michael's many close friends was Miles, Duke of Norfolk, and his family. The Duke and Duchess attended both the Requiem Services – at St Mary of the Angels and Westminster Cathedral, where the Duke read one of the readings. Anne, Duchess of Norfolk, was encouraged by Michael to ask us to publish a very special book by a patient in St Joseph's Hospice in Hackney, where she has very close associations in her role as patron. Bill Ellis had suffered an illness which damaged cells in his brain and left him totally paralysed, unable to move or speak. His mind and will were not affected and by the use of artificial aids he learnt

From left to right: Michael Hollings, Joan McCrimmon, Mary Craig and the Duke of Norfolk

to type and paint. The resulting book *The Long Road Back* was, in the words of Anne Norfolk, "a story of Resurrection and hope reborn."

In 1976 our Company was split in two as Kevin Mayhew decided to go it alone and I was left 'holding the baby' – quite literally, as Juliette my fourth child had just been born. During the early weeks and months after the split, Michael telephoned me almost daily, to encourage and help in any way he could. How often did I hear "Keep going. I'll pray." Without his strength the publishing company which is now called simply 'McCrimmons' would surely have disappeared.

Michael offered to write a book for the 'new' company and after a great deal of thought, I requested a spiritual autobiography. I was not alone in wanting to find out more about both Michael the person and the priest, and in so doing perhaps discover why his writing was so much in

143

demand. The book was called *Living Priesthood* – its importance in understanding Michael can be illustrated by the number of quotations taken from it in the other chapters of this book.

Living Priesthood was received with great enthusiasm – as our company scrapbook recorded. *The Church Times* declared that *Living Priesthood* was so called 'not to point out a contrast with dead priesthood, but because Fr Hollings gives us in this book the meaning of priesthood as he himself has progressively discovered it and tried to create it in the course of living.' John Coventry, writing in *The Tablet*, was particularly incisive.

> A priest can follow God's call to respond to, be open to, to get involved in every kind of human situation precisely in so far as he is involved in prayer. He can afford to tangle with the world and drop conventional protections and defences only in so far as he tangles with God in prayer. This twofold emphasis and giving of oneself is essential in the single process of becoming progressively human. It is for this reason that this book, quite apart from its reflections on issues of the day carries a revitalising message for any Christian. It is on this basis and attached, as it were, to this backbone, that Fr Hollings treats successively: prayer itself, sexuality, homosexuality, friendship, love, celibacy, marriage, healing and counselling, unlimited availability – particularly to the inadequate, community relations – first as a way of running a parish, ecumenical relations and race relations, the liturgy and sacraments and finally the 'open-house' policy of priestly ministry.

Michael wrote many other books for us in the twenty years left to him after *Living Priesthood*. One of my own special favourites was *The Shade of His Hand*, a compilation of prayers to help those facing illness and death and containing many offerings written by the sick and the dying themselves. Pocket size books such as *Prayers for the Depressed* and *Prayers before and after Bereavement* emerged from these larger collections. In addition, he compiled prayer books for communion and confirmation preparation, sacramental use and to help follow Mass each Sunday, while our final series of books by him was entitled *Reflections through the Church's Year* taken from his weekly parish newsletter. These newsletters were sent out far and wide, to his friends and many others, always with a short message such as 'Press on!' or 'Love and Prayers', and were carefully collected by Joan Cooley, who assisted Michael for so many years at St Mary of the Angels.

So much of Michael's own spirituality comes through in his writing. He spoke directly to God and encouraged us to do the same. He wrote as he prayed, in a simple way that we could all understand. He helped us to know God as a friend who could be approached without fuss and with complete honesty. Prayer for him was not only about making requests to God, it was about sharing our feelings, our fears, our guilt, our sadness, loss, anger and frustration. It was about coping with life's situations. Nor was it all doom and gloom – far from it. Prayer was very clearly also about celebrating life's joys and achievements, and giving thanks.

Michael was not only the Company's most successful writer. He was our adviser and friend – happy always to spend a day with us all at the seaside, throwing pebbles into the sea during the lunch break. And he was also our best customer, investing his royalties in hundreds of his books simply to give them away to parishioners and friends.

I have written this chapter from a personal perspective – because Michael was so important to us – and because I was his publisher for nearly three decades. But he spread the word elsewhere – and in many different ways.

Throughout his priestly life, Michael wrote regular columns for the religious press for the *Catholic Herald, The Universe* and other leading Christian papers. For instance, in 1959 he wrote a major Lenten series for *The Tablet*, 'At the Foot of the Cross'. His radio and television appearances spanned more than forty years. In the early days he took part in 'Dialogue Masses', often as commentator; as J. D. Crichton, the distinguished liturgist, wrote, he 'had just the right voice for the work – and what is more important – the right approach.' He spoke about prayer as he wrote about prayer. He broadcast about prayer often very late at night on television when most of us would be fast asleep in bed. And he

Michael with an altar boy before an ATV recording.

embraced new means of communication, as in his commentary on a delightful video *Dance To The Lord*, with children reflecting on spoken prayers in dance and song.

In addition, Michael mastered the art of the short homily, incisive and thought-provoking, delivering one every weekday Mass, and writing each week a reflection on the Sunday readings for his newsletter!

His diary was always full of invitations to preach, to give retreats, and to lecture. Invitations came from all over the world. He loved his visits to Ireland, the Caribbean, India, New Zealand, Australia and the United States, where he would meet up with his brother Tony, his sister-in-law Jennifer, and his two nephews and two nieces. And his telephone would never stop ringing; often I would visit him by appointment at St Mary of the Angels only to find my intended editorial meeting superseded by a more urgent call to 'spread the word'.

Two areas in which he did so with particular effect – through teaching, preaching and example – were those of Race Relations and Education. Mollie Lloyd, a friend of forty years and a Principal Lecturer in Multi-Cultural studies, has written movingly of how 'the quality of Michael's understanding and his intellectual outlook' led to his recognition by 'Christian, Hindu, Sikh and Muslim' as 'a holy man with a special mission to men and women of many races'. She recalls one Asian senior teacher in a High School in Southall saying simply, 'we know he is a holy man because he acts like one.'

Among the gifts that Michael Hollings left us was the example of his deep caring, his sharing of God's love for each of us and his willingness to listen. He would not readily give advice, but he would help those who sought his guidance to think through their need or problem themselves and pray to God for the answer. He gave completely of himself, asking nothing in return from those who sought his counsel. His teaching to so many of us, by example, was to get to know God better through prayer. How he found the time to help and care for so many was itself a miracle, for his friends ran into hundreds, if not thousands. He would never judge, he would simply encourage each one to keep going, press on and pray.

It was a great honour to be associated with Michael through his books, reaching out to a worldwide audience. I will never forget leaving his little room with all that wonderful 'mess' for the last time, clutching the final reflections for his last book, just days before he entered St Mary's hospital, in the autumn of 1996. Nor how we shared together, as we had so often shared before, a decade of the Rosary.

'Hail Mary...'

Joan McCrimmon met her husband James when they worked together in Repertory at Perth Theatre. She became a Catholic in 1957. The family moved to Southend in 1964 and in 1967 she co-founded the company now known as McCrimmons.

CHAPTER TEN

Teacher of Prayer

ELIZABETH REES

Michael was a man who could be irritable, pompous and hard to fathom. He was sometimes entrapped by his commitment. But he was made of prayer: he lived prayer and he breathed prayer. He was also one of the greatest teachers of prayer in our time, always searching for simpler language with which to invite people to pray, entice them to pray, urge them to pray. Michael was deeply in love with God, and he longed for others to fall in love with God as he had done.

At the age of 31, as a newly ordained priest, he began teaching others to pray through the printed word with a series of articles in *The Key*, the journal of a Catholic Action group. He begins with characteristic directness and enthusiasm:

> Hey You! Yes! You! Get things straight! Be what you are always talking about. Leaven the world. Start praying. Now! Without prayer, whatever springs from you will not flourish, any more than a tree will without roots. Unless you can see this – no, unless you can appreciate it sufficiently to practise prayer, you are in grave danger of wasting your energy…

> This is for you! Not for anyone else you can think of whom it would suit – it is for you! Now – go to it! Pray! When you are tired, pray the longer. It will seem endless, a useless waste of time. Excellent, for you could not be wasting it in a better way…

Later in the series, Michael returns to the challenge of how to become a person of prayer:

What then is recollection? It is the practice of a way of life, an attitude of mind, a disposition of heart, which leads us to turn back to God continually, wherever we are, whatever we are doing. It leads us from prayer and to prayer, permeating our existence with God-sense...

The first real fact is the hardest. This business of becoming a saint. Quite impractical, contrary to daily bread and income tax. Hard work? Ah, now we are at the basic reality! Yes, it is hard work, almost heroic work. For that reason it demands an enormous generosity, or willingness... The hard thing here and now is to realise we can only get a glimpse (of heaven) by wearing out our knees, reaching for God in darkness, desolation and a sense of intense stupidity.

It was in St Philip Neri that Michael discovered a model for his developing vision of a life open to God and open to others. He told me this in the 1960s, when he was first able to try out Philip Neri's idea of an open house and creative lifestyle. It is worth briefly reflecting on Philip Neri's life because Michael followed it in many ways. Philip Neri (1515–1595) was a Florentine who worked for a short while in commerce and then experienced a deep conversion. He went to Rome and lived in an attic as a hermit for a couple of years, paying his rent by tutoring his landlord's sons.

Philip Neri's attractive personality soon won him friends. He encouraged them to visit the sick with him, and gathered a group round him to look after pilgrims and those convalescing. He was ordained a priest and spent much of his time giving spiritual direction; he liked to spend nights praying in the catacombs. He gathered some friends together to live a common life without vows. The group largely consisted of those whom Philip Neri had helped by his advice and spiritual direction. People came to him in a constant stream: bishops, foreigners, the poor and the troubled. He was happy and considerate, and also a practical joker. One of his favourite phrases was *Non dubitare* – 'Don't worry'. Those who know Michael will recognise in the story of Philip Neri many of the elements of the lifestyle which Michael created, both at the Chaplaincy in Oxford and in his parishes of Southall and Bayswater: the many friends, the stream of visitors, shared living, spiritual direction and deep prayer.

149

As an assistant curate, Michael had no opportunity to try out Philip Neri's lifestyle. He wrote in *St Patrick's Missionary Magazine* of his first parish in Soho:

> The front door was guarded by two 'dragonesses'... They felt their duty was to safeguard the priests from importunate callers at the door or on the phone. As a young priest this frustrated me... Jesus came for us, to live among us, to be with us, to be available. Two words, open and available, penetrated me and irritated my inner being. I did not know how to do it, but I desperately wanted at least a sense of greater openness to people.

Throughout his life, the words open and available were close to Michael's heart. He always sought to be open and available to people and to God, and he continually encouraged those around him to live in the same way. In 1959, when Michael became Chaplain at Oxford University, he was able to live more fully his ideal of being open and available to God and to others. Prayer was the cornerstone of his new life. He slept, as he said, 'from two to five, twice a day'. He took holidays on the Isle of Man, where he walked by the sea and wrote books on prayer with his Anglican friend, Etta Gullick. He would return to Oxford on the overnight train and be in chapel, as usual, early in the morning.

When I first met Michael in 1969, I was a shy undergraduate entering the big, unknown world of Oxford University. I had left the certainties of home and school and come to St Hilda's College to read music. The college was a caring and supportive environment, but somehow it never became 'home' for me because Michael got in first. Over the years, he gathered around him a motley praying 'family' of all kinds of people, for whom the Old Palace was home. The Old Palace was always open, and there were boiled eggs for breakfast for anyone who came to the early morning Mass in the Nissen hut which then served as a chapel.

What was Michael's impact on me during my three years at college? For a long time I felt overawed. Michael's example of prayer and his gift for creating a Christian community were very evident and deeply attracted me, yet they also overpowered me. Michael was basically a shy person who did not normally initiate a relationship. I wanted to learn more about praying, but for a whole year I was simply afraid to approach Michael. Finally, with a fellow student's encouragement I managed to do so. For the next two years I went to Michael once a week for spiritual direction. The pattern was always the same: after Mass and breakfast at the Old Palace, I would climb the rickety stairs to chat with Michael, sitting on the faded red sofa which had been his bed the night before. Neither of us spoke much, but he listened intently and understood everything I struggled to say. Michael always empowered me, yet he could be quite directive. He brought me to a place of great freedom.

As increasing numbers of people learned from Michael how to pray, he was increasingly asked to give retreats. His input was practical rather than pious. Recently, when I asked an elderly Benedictine monk what he could remember about a retreat which Michael had led in his monastery forty years ago, he told me, 'Michael's advice about prayer was: "Get on with it!".' Ordinary Catholics didn't really talk much about prayer in the 1960s, but Michael wanted his college students to have every opportunity to pray, so he regularly offered evening courses on prayer at the Catholic Chaplaincy.

He evolved a simple and clear teaching style. The more he tried to convey what prayer meant to him, the more he fielded a wide range of questions. His talks to students eventually emerged as a book entitled *Day by Day*, published by Mayhew-McCrimmon in 1972. Despite its unassuming title, it is one of the clearest and most compelling guidebooks on prayer. Michael was not afraid to share his personal experience as he described the praying person's journey:

> In the beginning, I did an awful lot of work myself, and felt the time given, the tiredness, the battle with sleep, the distractions all worthwhile... This in turn gave way to a rhythm like breathing which is essential, yet not often realised in day to day to living. And so, for me, over a

151

period of years, the intangible depth which is relationship, friendship, devotion and love all rolled into one, has gone on unfolding and enfolding until it has become unthinkable that I should stop living prayer. This is not to say that there is always a clear consciousness of God's loving presence, no time for pain, doubt or further disillusion. All these are possible and part of the variegated pattern. But it does now seem as though to stop praying would be to stop breathing and living all at the same moment (pp13-14).

Michael knew that prayer required perseverance:

The approach to God is not all that easy, and therefore it is something that we have to work away at... I do not want to make you feel that it is desperately hard, but I would suggest that discipline is part of the general way of our living, though perhaps I am wrong about this. However, it would seem to me that anybody who is going to get anywhere in life... has to have a certain amount of discipline. I do not believe that pictures just get painted. I do not believe, on the whole, people just turn into wonders in the world of music, that it just happens to them. They have to practise regularly and hard. I do not believe that books just get written in a flash overnight. It does not happen that way. There is a very real need for discipline, and this applies to prayer as well (pp.18, 36).

Michael encouraged a daily chunk of prayer, balanced by using all the day's odd moments to return to our relationship with God:

I have certainly found that the best time to be alone with God, as a single person, is early in the morning, simply because not everyone else likes getting up early in the morning or bothers you at that particular time... Part of the discipline, just like learning how much sleep you need, is learning to take and make use of the odd couple of minutes or five minutes with which each of our days is littered (pp.38, 41).

For Michael, all this was a means to 'let God get at you', to allow God to get well mixed into your life:

And now, a final aspect of this. I would call it allowing yourself, being disciplined in yourself, to be 'pickled in God'. By that I mean that you accept God around you, in you, penetrating you and conditioning you... and believe this is going on, even when there is little or no evidence that this is the case (pp.42-43).

Michael constantly struggled to find simple ways to convey what happens in prayer. He used the image of looking at your own hand:

> Draw it slowly towards you. At first you can keep it in focus, and then gradually it is too close to be seen whole and clearly. Finally, it is right up against your face and you cannot see at all... everything is dark... but the contact is very real and very different... Well, the same reaction occurs in the relationship with God. The closer we approach, the more dark is our knowledge. When a person is set down before God, is trying hard to be recollected, is even trying to think of God and Christ, and all that happens is that there is a blank, an emptiness, a pain, it is not easy to get across to that person that all is well and this is as it should be. BUT IT IS AS IT SHOULD BE! (pp.95-96).

However, it is important to remember that God does most of the work:

> About ninety per cent of all prayer in a person is the work of God: only some ten per cent is the work of the person concerned... When this fact is accepted, the transition from active to passive in prayer is that much easier... It is probably only by faith that a person can hold himself in stillness and openness and joy, when nothing seems to happen at all. And it is at this point that the leap forward can take place, God intervening, provided that we have the courage to remain in his apparent absence and accept his presence, until such time as he makes it clear to us that this is worthwhile. Mind you, this is not easy, and it does take quite a lot of self-discipline, patience and the humility of accepting being blankly stupid. Quickly or slowly, but certainly surely, the Spirit will invade and take over, in a darkness which has been described as dazzling, in the white light of radiant joy, in the stillness of complete tranquillity (pp.97,98).

Much of the time, though, prayer can seem routine and boring. A prayer-guide is helpful, to make sense of what is going on:

You don't even know if you are coming or going, you don't know if you are going backwards or forwards. At least this is not quite true, as part of you does know. But it is necessary to have some human reassurance because it does seem to be so strange (pp.106-107).

Such prayer brings peace, but not perfection:

You are still going to get ratty, still going to get tired, still going to be ill... However, I think it is true to say that a certain tranquillity does pervade, and that there is a certain sense of depth, a sureness and peace... Contemplation and the way of life it involves is very demanding, but it is worth all the risks, the pain, the struggles, the hard work it may entail, for by it the love of God can grow and work in us in a most wonderful and all embracing way (pp.109, 113).

Michael left Oxford and became Parish Priest of Southall in 1970. In this quite different environment, he now kept in touch by letter with many of the people who had initially come to him wanting to pray, but the focus of his work now shifted, as he searched for ways to share the prayer of his Moslem and Sikh neighbours, and to create living liturgy for his Catholic parish. His people were a roughly equal mix of Anglo-Irish, Afro-Caribbeans and Asians. When I stayed in the presbytery one Pentecost weekend, parishioners were writing 'Come, Holy Spirit' on large paper strips in a bewildering variety of alphabets, to pin to the curtains that hung round the entire apse wall. That night there were race riots, and Michael typically forbade us to go onto the streets, while he went out to see how he could be of help.

Michael encouraged creative liturgy at Southall. One Holy Week when I was staying in the presbytery, the Palm Sunday procession began in the school grounds, where the young celebrant in a white alb mounted a donkey and rode through the streets to the church. A joyful procession surrounded him, with Sheila Cassidy at the donkey's head with a carrot, in case the donkey needed enticing in the right direction. A parishioner hovered in the church car park with a dustpan and brush in case of accidents. As the celebrant rode down the aisle towards the sanctuary, someone had an epileptic fit; Sheila Cassidy changed into doctor mode and tended the person in the sacristy. The Gospels came alive in Southall's liturgy.

With some difficulty, Michael tried to transpose his open-house lifestyle from a university setting to the parish presbytery. Now that he was working once more within the diocese, he came in contact with a great many diocesan clergy, and began to work on the book *Living Priesthood*, from which a generation of priests took inspiration. Almost immediately, he tackled the subject closest to his heart, with a chapter on the centrality of prayer:

> The centre and core of the whole priestly life is the relationship with God... I mean that this relationship is to be so deep, strong and all pervading that it is the very pulse, lifeblood, heart of his whole being... Day by day, summer, winter, spring, autumn, rain or fine, time must be given lavishly to God. By this I do not mean simply the total giving of life in a generalised way, but also solid giving of personal time each day... Neglect of pastoral work is not in fact the outcome, because the deepening knowledge and love of God through prayer drives the person out from the solitude and depth of union to a zest for spending himself on God's people. Time and again, I have come across just such a person – not only among priests – and their impact is electric (pp.43, 47, 48).

Michael again encourages the combination of a daily chunk of prayer with a continuous drip-feed approach:

> Prayer could and can often be sleepy-stupid, but it is important to remember that it is God who is doing the work, and that the brightest of my thoughts pales into insignificance in the light of his revelation. My part is to be there, to be willing, and to try to be open. A man is often most vulnerable to God in tiredness and on the borders of sleep...

> It is possible to build a web of prayer which takes some spinning, but is then embracing and pervading. 'Contact' with God is then of such a consistency that though work, play, conversation and many other occupations seem to drive the thought of God from us, his abiding presence is

made clear by the ease with which he returns to our minds and hearts at moments of stillness, waiting or rest. As with a person deeply in love with his wife, who will feel a closeness and warmth, without even first consciously adverting to her, so this experience of loving and being loved wells up from the depth of our being (p.49).

I came to know Michael best in his final parish of St Mary of the Angels, in Bayswater. I joined him there as pastoral assistant in 1980, and lived and worked alongside him for the next six years. I still felt awed by his closeness to God, and it required some courage for me to ask to become his assistant. In those early days of consultation of the laity, Michael already had a parish team and a parish council, and it was typical of Michael that he consulted both groups before letting me come to join him. The members of the parish team were not hand-picked professionals but a mixture of volunteers, deacons-in-training, foreign priests trying to learn English, young offenders on pre-prison release and recovering alcoholics, among others. Michael delighted in creating community out of the most motley crew imaginable. This sprang from his persistent belief in people's innate goodness. The parish house reminded me of the chaos at the dawn of time, out of which creation might or might not emerge. So with our parish team: some people grew into themselves, while others remained in chaos. Michael gave each of them every possible chance to grow, and in this way we staggered on. Many found the lifestyle intolerable; some of us enjoyed it, and Michael thrived on it.

Michael's day was disciplined, like that of any soldier. He went down to church at 5am for an hour's prayer, wrapped in his cloak in winter, torch in hand. The house was quiet as I followed him downstairs each day. This time of prayer was the bedrock of his ministry and mine. It also forged a silent bond between us as month by month the ship of our parish weathered the storms that came our way. At 6am Michael unlocked the church and we climbed the stairs to the kitchen where Doris, the housekeeper, was now making coffee for breakfast for fifteen people. Charlie, the handyman, had by now arrived from Catford, having set out in his old minibus an hour earlier, before the morning traffic. As we drank coffee and joked and laughed before the working day began, Michael prepared soup for the daily bread-and-cheese lunch. He now had time to write letters, take early morning phone calls and give spiritual direction before Morning Prayer, Mass and breakfast.

Michael found new ways for his parish, and indeed the whole neighbourhood, to come together in prayer. He had a great sense of celebration and of theatre, and with his commanding personality, he could draw the whole community together. In Holy Week every third year, the Kensington Churches produced a Way of the Cross through the streets, a powerful piece of street theatre. Scenes from the life and passion of Jesus were acted in costume at different spots along the route. Cardinal Hume and various bishops, Anglican and Catholic, led meditations from balconies of selected residents' homes. One year a marching band led us from place to place. There were also hymns; one year, dressed as a first century Palestinian, I sang 'Steal away to Jesus', amplified up and down Portobello Road.

When we had selected the housing estate which was to form the backdrop for the Crucifixion, residents were leafleted to ask them to extinguish their lights during the Crucifixion. Nearer the time, a giant scaffold was erected for the crosses. The actual event was deeply moving. I can still see two barefooted young women, recently baptized, following Christ the prisoner through the streets, spontaneously crying, 'We love you, Jesus!' The weather could be terrible. A thunderstorm accompanied the Crucifixion one year, and the good thief was taken to hospital with hypothermia. Jesus was taken down from the cross relatively unscathed, and the resurrection was celebrated with fireworks in a park on the next housing estate.

With such powerful religious experiences, and many smaller ones in the course of a year, many people found new meaning in their lives. Frequently at our evening Mass someone would be received into the

Church, to be welcomed to supper in the parish house afterwards with their family. In the 1980s, such people were normally instructed individually; this suited Michael's personal style, and also suited the very diverse kinds of people who asked to join the Church. Michael's way of preparing people to enter the Church was highly individualistic: he listened to each person's particular needs and responded to them. He handed on to me a Malaysian trainee accountant whom he had been instructing. Since the young man was Buddhist, there was in fact a lot for him to learn. Michael told me: 'We've had about six sessions. I've mostly been helping him with maths, which he finds very difficult to do in English; he's got exams coming up. Just give him a few more sessions, and we'll fix a date to receive him into the Church.' Such an approach might shock religious educators, but the young man was deeply touched by Michael's sensitivity to his needs, and fifteen years on I can still remember the magnificent celebratory meal with which the Malaysian student community marked his entry into the Church.

Many people came to him for confession or spiritual direction. One parishioner recalls: 'Michael was my sounding board. He listened while I turned from worm to butterfly. I can honestly say he never gave me any advice – which is, no doubt, in a nutshell, the essence of the wonder of his gift. He never let you stop with him, but always pointed you on to God; he never allowed himself to get in the way'. Great numbers of people came to Michael for advice on how to pray and how to live, but Michael limited his time with his many visitors. You rarely had more than half an hour with Michael, and if you seemed to require less, he'd say: 'I'm going to throw you out now'. He'd finish the session, perhaps with a Hail Mary, get up, show you the door, and wander round the house to see what wanted to happen next. He kept in touch with a great many people by sending them brief letters of advice and encouragement, and he kept in touch with still more by sending them the weekly parish bulletin, with a personal message scribbled at the top. He was a master of spiritual direction through the written word, though his scrawl was always difficult to decipher, written very fast, and now with failing eyesight.

Michael was perhaps old-fashioned in his extensive use of letters rather than the telephone, but for him, letters too were a channel of grace and something tangible to which a recipient could return for strength. In a letter, Michael shared his feelings more easily than he could face to face. Later, in a difficult working situation, I wrote to Michael asking whether or not to let the pain of the situation get mixed up into my prayer. His reply was:

> Bury yourself in God's love, but you cannot be an ostrich! I'm afraid, to me, it seems that you see the reality and truth of the situation, and you bear the pain of it with Jesus. That is easier said than done. But you have taken on work for the Lord, and serving him with X but not for X in the deep sense. If we live for Jesus, then the pain does not necessarily grow less, as you know. But it is somehow bearable. I have, myself, never been able to shut out pain or disruption or attack or neglect. I have to live with them because I cannot get rid of them!...

Later I moved into work in a retreat centre, where life was less pressured and more centred. I queried with Michael whether it was all right to be doing less work. Again, he drew a parallel with his own journey. He wrote:

> I am very glad to get your report on yourself. Keep it like that. It is very good for you to be quieter. To love and serve God fully and deeply we do not have to be frenetic! I'm learning day by day how I have to do less. The trouble is that it means I should be more. Learn with me. Lovely things happen as you know even in powerlessness! It is interesting facing my situation of having eighteen months to go before I am retired at 75. I'm gradually shedding things. Interesting! Pray I have the grace to grow less as He grows more!

After Michael's removal from the parish and his reinstatement, he still pressed on with courage. He wrote to me:

> Cardinal Hume reinstated me yesterday. I am now back at St Mary's. Pray thanks and also pray for me for strength to go on and develop a bit further!

Michael continued bravely on his journey to God. He wrote his last letter to me on Boxing Day 1996, in his final illness. He ended with:

> Liz, I can't write much. I'm in hospital – diabetes problems. Now trying to 'mend'! Very hard work with physiotherapy and wounds to heal. I came in 11th Oct! Now ops over – but I am having to learn to walk again – not easy. I am very weak! Can only stand at a zimmer if helped and need someone to stand behind me even so. I will be here weeks the doctor says. Pray hard. I need courage, patience, strength and power to live in the PRESENT moment. My love, and God bless you. Michael.

This was Michael's constant struggle and constant desire: to live in the present moment, and to live each moment to the full. Along the way he sought and received the courage, patience, strength and power to do so.

Sr Elizabeth Rees OCV worked for fifteen years as a pastoral assistant in parishes in and around London. More recently, she has worked on retreat teams, and is currently at the Ammerdown Retreat and Conference Centre, Radstock, Bath. She is a writer, counsellor and spiritual director.

CHAPTER ELEVEN

'Just Being Around'

ALEXANDER SHERBROOKE

How often it is said of someone – 'as they lived so they died'. Those words speak to me of an almost unnoticed scene outside Westminster Cathedral on the day of Michael's funeral. There had been much grieving, and also, as Michael would have liked, celebrating, at the Vigil Mass in St Mary's the night before, ushering in the quiet and the remembering of the night vigil. The following morning the hearse brought his body down to Victoria, but it made better progress than expected, leaving the undertakers quite some time to waste before the start of the Mass. They used it to slip away for some refreshment, leaving the hearse and Michael's mortal remains seemingly abandoned. Many would have said 'how disrespectful of the dead' (to which no doubt he would have retorted, 'what nonsense dear! I am not there!') However, it left one of Michael's dearest friends of many years, who had been refused access to St Mary's intensive care unit, the chance to spend twenty minutes alone with his old friend and confidante. He described it as a moment of great peace; 'it was as though Michael was very, very close to me and I was able to say goodbye until I meet him again'.

In those last few months, so full of physical and emotional pain, both in and outside the Parish, and latterly in hospital, Michael taught so much to those who met him. It was as though that period underlined and explained all that he had tried to share with us in the more proactive part of his ministry. So much of his life had been spent 'rushing' – there was never a dull moment when he was around – but what underpinned everything was his all-consuming love of God and his desire for God to use him as an agent of love. Any thought, action, word spoken, or innocuous gesture offered, could be used by God. St Thérèse of Lisieux, such an inspiration to him for so much of his life, had taught him to be the form, the pattern and the means for God to be present in the world, and never to query, question or measure how useless or worthwhile any action might be. Watching Michael's great hulk of a body battling in the intensive care unit, spying the breviary in his hospital room or his friend saying goodbye outside the Cathedral, shows what it means to be a child of God – for in the 'uselessness' of those moments God was at work. For Michael that was all that was necessary.

As diocesan priests the Church invites us to be ready to touch and engage with all areas of life, whether it be sacramental moments from the cradle to the grave, the finance and administration of the parish, social agencies engaged with the local community, or the life of prayer to God for the needs of his people. Michael was no exception – whether it was marriage preparation, the Notting Hill Carnival Committee, early morning meditation, or making sandwiches and that Michaelish soup for 'the gentlemen of the road'. Most of us compare figures of how many funerals we have celebrated or meetings attended that week. Michael never joined in with that kind of conversation because he never spoke about his work, but also because somehow that work seemed to be a reflection of something else. All Michael desired was to be a faithful steward of God's purposes; and in that he saw the sick and dying as pointing the way because of their privileged proximity to the Redeeming Christ.

I believe that it was in his work with the sick and the dying that we can find a leitmotif for his work as an ordained priest – because it is in this work that we most profoundly touch both the mystery of God's presence among us, and conversely also his radical absence. To stay with the sick and the dying one must have great humility and acceptance because all that is human in us wants to understand and explain, to measure and judge, and to package, so we can rush on to the next thing and not waste time. Yet, as Michael wrote – 'It is important to anyone who is reading this to sit and seriously consider his or her attitude to death and dying. Please do this. The happiness of yourself and perhaps quite a number of others depends upon your openness'.(1) Similarly, very often he would scribble in a book given, or newsletter sent, 'Love Him because He loves you', and perhaps here too is another way into his sharing with the sick and dying. Michael was in love with a personal God who listens to us and who calls us to listen to him, even though to do so flies in the face of all of our behavioural patterns, for normally we want to do, to judge, to act, and above all to control. Listening requires us to sit still and consciously to resist the distraction of restlessness – so necessary if we are to find God in the most forsaken and abandoned. We are reassured in the words Michael would drum in to those who would go to him for advice – 'just be around'.

It is impossible to give chapter and verse for everything Michael did, although I suspect the gratitude and love of the people at St Mary's and at the Cathedral at the time of his death could do that better than anything else. Certainly being with those who were trapped in poverty, sickness, death or bereavement seemed natural to him. I would like to offer three reflections that give something of an insight into Michael's solidarity with them.

The first concerns Michael's relationship with his mother. In his room in front of his desk, there was a gracious antique chair seemingly more inviting to piles of papers than it was to a sedentary visitor. He had few personal possessions, but this chair, which had belonged to her, along with her photograph on the mantelpiece, always seemed to be the most conspicuous of them. I suspect that his mother's battle with cancer, and her death, marked him more deeply than even his closest friends would suspect. Towards the end of the Second World War the amalgamation of the two battalions of the Coldstream Guards meant that only one adjutant of the two was allowed home on leave. Both seemed equally deserving

---

1 *Alive to Death* p28

cases. One adjutant was a husband with a wife and four children; the other, Michael, had a mother who was terminally ill. Michael gave the leave ticket to his fellow adjutant and stayed on. He was, in fact, able to make a brief trip later on, but by then his mother needed serious nursing and was approaching her end. By the time she died Michael was in Palestine, unable to get permission to return for the funeral. For him this period of intense grieving somehow helped him to rediscover his lost faith; 'It had the effect of crystallising God's rediscovery of me, as I tried to reassess myself and life after war, after her death'.(2) Both war with all its attendant horrors and personal loss can be crippling assaults on a person's faith – but for Michael the latter seems to have led to a rediscovery of the love of God in, and also despite, darkness. Although he would refrain from talking much about it, it had all thrown him onto God. Contact with sickness and death not only takes us into the mystery of the Cross but also tests how patient our love is.

Michael would often talk about the importance of 'sharing'; a word easily mocked but so redolent of the patience of walking with someone in an illness, not preaching but listening, being honest with and not hiding in secrecy – all hallmarks of Michael. It is much easier to pigeonhole the whole business and to quote the wisdom of others, than simply to wait, listen and share one's vulnerability. Michael's particular sorrow at not being present at his mother's death led him to speak and write unceasingly about being with those who were dying. For him, that intense moment of loneliness was also the greatest moment of humanity and was often the one that was remembered when other memories faded. It is surely God who explains man to himself and it is in that hidden meeting or death that strangely we are most alive. Michael would walk it many times and in so doing brought and shared much comfort and love to and from grieving relations and friends. It is for Christians a moment of triumph when we can sing with St Paul, 'Death, where is your victory?' and it is where we experience in the profoundest sense both the mystery of God's abundant and overflowing presence, and, paradoxically, His absence. Michael did not write much about his sadness at not being at his mother's, death but the loss was in some way compensated for by the way he taught so many others to be present at the deathbeds of those they loved.

The second concerns his work in Lourdes. Jean Buscail has worked for the Hospitalité there for over forty-three years, the vast majority of which have been spent in the airport, where he is now the *chef de brancardiers*. Jean, would not, I think, mind being called a spiritual son of Michael for it was Michael who helped him become the man he is today. Michael, when physically active, devoted much of his spare time to working for the Hospitalité, and I believe that there almost more than anywhere else – in the witness he gave, and the love

Michael in Lourdes whilst filming for ATV, 1958

he shared – he was able to lead many into the priesthood and the religious life. Working in the airport was either feast or famine, often waiting many hours for a delayed plane to arrive, or else coping with a great outpouring of humanity, tired, uncomfortable, delayed and eager for their hospital bed. Jean remembers Michael as very much part of a team, with no airs or graces and ready to share the load with others. He was always matted with sweat but concerned only to give the sick the care and the love that Christ would give. He would always handle them with great delicacy, as if conscious that they were the suffering Christ, but unlike many, he was reluctant to engage in conversation unless the sick asked for it. The silence of listening was always enough for him for it was here that Christ was to be met. The hours of waiting, often in the early hours of the morning, would see Michael walking up and down with his Rosary, preparing himself for both the Garden of Gethsemane and the Resurrection, the mysteries which somehow explain the folly that is Lourdes.

Lourdes can easily invite a cynical response from the occasional tourist both for the shops with their glitzy and kitsch souvenirs, and for the morbidity of the baths and everything engendered therein. Intentionally or not, the baths are sepulchral and uninviting, the water very cold and suspicious. Nevertheless it is to the baths that many pilgrims have travelled in answer to Our Lady's request. Here the skill and delicacy of undressing the sick and preparing them for 'the tomb' have to be second to none. Watching and working with volunteers can be a great example of the love and the care that God wants us to envelop His suffering body with. The bath is a baptismal experience; so full of death in its cold murkiness and inhospitableness, but also so blest by God in the graces, love, peace and life that the bather radiates as he or she 'rises' from the water. It was here that over many years Michael met the intimate reality of death so quickly snatched away and replaced by the great promise of immortality. Here, too, was a communal experience, one in which the helpers shared as they would in surrounding the bed of a dying person or helping to plan the funeral rites of a loved one. So long as he had the strength and the mobility to engage with it, this place was for Michael a touching of, and by, God. Once it defeated him physically, God would need him elsewhere.

The third area was the vineyard of the Parish where Michael grew ever more unstinting in his service. Melissa, for example, before she moved into the Bon Secours home, was visited on Friday with the Catholic papers and Parish newsletter; on Saturday, Michael cooked her a meal, and on Sunday he brought her the Lord in Holy Communion. One year when she had become almost blind he wrote all her Christmas cards. In itself this might seem nothing much out of the ordinary but it needs to be set alongside the newsletters with which Michael would keep in contact with a whole range of disparate 'little Christs' (to use St Camillus' expression), his total availability for the sick, dying and grieving; and the light on the second floor which never seemed to go out; moreover, Michael was always ready to share his time and to celebrate Mass in the house of the housebound. There might seem to be nothing remarkable in this, simply a pastor being diligent about the care of his flock, but when lived and fed by prayer, it gained an extra dimension. Michael in his prayer learnt not only to listen and meet God but also to experience His radical silence. This was especially vivid in his sharing with the sick and dying – 'Just being around'. Perhaps this state of readiness, what the Italians would call '*disponibilità*' – availability – was what made him always so ready to face a new situation or confront a new challenge whether it was the Notting Hill Carnival Committee, the voice of women in the Church, or the scourge of AIDS. Ever youthful, Michael never seemed to grow crusty with age or cynical in his seniority, and he remained always ready to go to the suffering Christ wherever He should appear. In the 1980's, AIDS struck with a particular force in North Kensington. Michael responded in a truly evangelical way, ready to pass over any of the shibboleths or taboos that should get in his path. Judging was not part of the game – pastorally, and in the context of spiritual direction, he would meet people 'where they were at', but also leave them with the perennial challenge, 'Press on'.

Cardinal Hume, in his sermon at Michael's funeral at Westminster Cathedral, listed and applauded some of Michael's characteristics – and then added: 'but Michael I can hear you saying 'Stop, stop!'. Michael would say in all of this there's nothing remarkable here, I was simply being faithful in my mission'. Of course that was true, but again, there was a further quality that helps to complete the picture, something to do with timelessness. Priests tend always to be looking at their watch. Michael's day was carefully advertised on the daily timetable 'Michael… 10.00 Mass, 10.30–11.00 Interview, 11.00–12.00 Marks and Spencers,

12.00–1.00 pm Priest to Priest' and so on – but you never felt he was rushing you, nor would he, a stickler for punctuality, ever be late. I believe there was a real sense that Michael was so in love with God, so aware of His presence, that God's time became Michael's time. Michael loved the sick and the dying because they taught him how to wait and to listen and, above all, how to be alone with God. The phrase from the psalm, 'Be still and know that I am God' can and does sell shelves of spiritual books, but in the reality of incarnational living, it is the most difficult to practise simply because it requires us to confront that which is most certain – namely that we sin and that we will die. Conversely, dying is the most intimate moment of living – and yet Michael throughout died to live.

Michael was of a generation of priests and lay people who found it natural to follow in the Little Way of St Thérèse. But what appealed wasn't the spirituality of the kitsch statue or soupy language of adulation – rather it was her straightforward matter-of-factness. She taught a way of loving that all can live but which required that one first unite oneself to her obedience and faithfulness. She only wanted to love with the heart of Jesus, unquestioning and accepting. This made her patient in love; as Michael wrote "If you truly love God, the pain does not go away – but you live more fully". We cannot be what we are not and we have to love where Christ has put us. Michael loved a myriad of people of all kinds and types and what made sense of that love was his knowledge of the stillness and quietness of a listening God. He listened himself which made him at ease with 'Just being around' those to whom God listens most – the poor, the outcast, the sick and the dying. Perhaps the final words about this wonderful man, who lived rather than owned his priesthood, are words of his own:

> It may be pain... just stay here... it helps...
> It may be loneliness... I'm afraid... don't go away...
> It may be despair... I'm so empty... I'm in a panic... Help me!
> It may be peace... stay quietly with me, and speak of God.

It may be love... I love you so much. I can do nothing...
but be here.

I just hope and pray that what is written here will convey something to
you. If it is something felt and responded to, thank God.

If it is disbelief... pray.

If it is a feeling I have got it all wrong... write and tell me so.

For I want to put before you the full humanity of man, woman and child,
as shown in the real Jesus Christ... God and Man... because:

Although he was Son, he learnt to obey through suffering; but having
been made perfect, he became for all who obey him the source of eternal salvation... (Hebrews. 5:8-10) (3)

*Alexander Sherbrooke spent his diaconate year with Michael at St Mary of
the Angels and was ordained there in September 1988. He is now parish
priest of St Margaret's, Twickenham.*

---

3 Ibid, pp12-13

CHAPTER TWELVE

A Way of the Cross

JOCK DALRYMPLE

In Michael's first letter to his cousin Jock, written in early 1949 when they were both studying in Rome, he expressed himself thus:

> ...it is excellent to think that you are happy at the Scots College – a very excellent thing indeed.
>
> But as you know, happiness is not everything and God is usually very good about letting us down lightly. You have been very generous in giving up your life to him; and he will always outdo you in generosity. But giving is a continual job and he just wants to see it all the time, in joy and sorrow. When the time comes and everything is quite black and impossible and there is every reason for not carrying on, that is just the time when God is showing you most love, and by hanging on you are showing most love to Him. But of course one of the main trials is that we cannot see that at the time.

Nearly fifty years later, I don't think that Michael any longer held the view that our times of darkness are the times when God is showing us most love – but he certainly continued to prize the virtues of perseverance and endurance. And not only did he prize them, he lived them, especially in the last eighteen months of his life.

The events of those months have been referred to earlier in this book. Paul Milanowski wrote of how, 'stigmatised by public accusation', Michael 'was forced to remove himself from the people he loved and served.', and then to endure 'months of suffering in silence and obedience, prayer and loneliness, in a state of rapid physical decline.' Indeed,

Roderick Strange was led to comment that Michael's final gift to him might well have been 'the lesson that those who follow the Master may be asked to die in darkness.'

The months of darkness began in September 1995. On September 2nd, Michael concelebrated the Nuptial Mass of Annabelle Richardson and Donald McCrimmon, Joan's son, at the Church of St Mary the Virgin in Hambledon, near Henley, giving a simple but telling homily on the meaning and sharing of God's love. He had prepared himself with a quiet time of prayer in the Lady Chapel and slipped away to another appointment shortly after the ceremony.

If Michael seemed particularly reflective that afternoon, it was because he had already been alerted to the accusing headlines that were to appear the following morning in the *News of the World*. A man alleged that some twenty-five years earlier, when he was seventeen, Michael had molested him while he had been staying at St. Anselm's in Southall. Within a few days and in keeping with standard procedures, Michael was placed on 'administrative leave' while first the church authorities, and then the police, made investigations.

Michael had to move out of the presbytery and found a home not far away with his close friend, Freda Berkeley, widow of the composer, Lennox Berkeley. His name appeared elsewhere in the national and religious press. It hurt. So did the wide berth given him throughout the months that followed by some in the Church.

He made no attempt publicly to respond to the allegations. Nor would he allow his friends to do so on his behalf. At first he suffered greatly from the uncertainty, writing to me in late September: 'I have no news. Just keep praying. I am in an uncomfortable limbo.' As time went on, aided by Freda's kindness and sensitivity, he adapted, beginning to see people again and to keep up his remarkable correspondence, sometimes ending letters with the simple request, 'pray for me and the continuing "due process"'.

At no point did his faith waver. He rose to pray, as he had always done so, at four o'clock every morning. He celebrated Mass every day. He prayed his breviary.

Early in 1996, the police indicated that there was no basis for any action to be taken. Cardinal Hume went to St Mary's on Sunday, February 18th and announced that Michael was resuming work as parish priest, to the spontaneous acclaim of the parishioners. Michael himself returned the following day.

Soon he was joined by Fr Mark Langham. Before the allegations it had been expected that Michael would stand down as parish priest on his 75th birthday, at the end of December. Now it was agreed with the Cardinal that he would stay on until Easter 1997, when Mark would succeed him.

On one level, Michael took up where he had left off. One of those who kept in touch with him during the previous five months received this letter, written on February 28th.

> A short line to express to you something of my deep appreciation of all your loving care and concern during the period of my exile from the parish. It was for me a tremendous support that you were getting on with God's work and praying for me. It was a painful, remarkable and growthful period for me. I hope I have learnt to trust the Lord more. Now I am tired by over-much publicity. I pray it will end soon. Everyone has been very kind in welcoming me back, but some almost too kind. I want to say nothing and be low profile.
>
> Thank you again, deeply. My love and prayer. God bless you.

However, the events of the previous months had taken their toll; Michael was walking more slowly and tiring more easily, and was more prone to bouts of illness. On 4th April, Maundy Thursday, he wrote to me: 'Sorry to have been out of touch. I have found it quite hard work – and now have got a bug – squitters, vomiting and lack of balance - plus a lot of calls, people for direction etc. All lovely except the sickness. Newsletter not yet done…'

In the late summer, Mother Teresa visited London. During his Southall years, Michael had invited her and her sisters into his parish to set up what became the first Missionary of Charity community in Britain. Thereafter whenever she came to England, she would always ask for 'Fr Michael' to celebrate a six o'clock morning Mass. Poignantly, their last conversation was of how they would meet next in heaven. (1)

In some ways, it seemed as though Michael had been freed a little more. He had always been ambivalent about public esteem. Now, in the aftermath of perceived 'scandal', he knew that things would never be the same again. It was as if he had been stripped, prepared for the last stage of the journey to God. He had always believed that the followers of Jesus shared in his death and resurrection and that its pattern was marked out in their lives as well as in the pages of the Gospels. The Way of the Cross became ever more his way, too.

For many years he had slept too little and driven himself too hard in order to serve the Lord and his people. Physically this took its toll. On October 11th, he was taken into hospital, St Mary's, Paddington. Ulcers in his leg, aggravated by diabetes, stubbornly refused to heal. With his retirement in sight, he was particularly desperate to get better quickly and return to St. Mary of the Angels, but to no avail. In early November he wrote:

> ...I am being more long term than I hoped. The doctors cannot say how long it will take to heal...the surgeon and doctors are pleased with the toe and foot, not so pleased with the back of knee and veins... As they are just waiting and hoping it is all I can do too. Probably be at least two more weeks...

Two weeks later, he was still there.

> ...My situation is that I am presently mostly in bed. I am also in isolation – having a bug that is resistant to antibiotics. But the general trend is very good. The head surgeon today said that the left foot was excellent. I can begin putting weight on it. The leg and veins have been a nui-

---

1 Mother Teresa died in September 1997, six months after Michael.

sance because they have not healed properly, but he was very confident today that they were much improved and were healing – but it will take time – neither he nor anyone knows, but it seems more likely to be weeks than days.

...The Cardinal came to see me yesterday – very kind. I told him NOT to come again – much too much to do – and I was praying for him. He agreed and left shortly after.

Fr Mark Langham is doing a good job at St Mary's and is much liked there, which is excellent.

Clearly I do not know how long I will be here, but it will be healing and then beginning to walk again and getting generally stronger.

I don't find I can read much serious stuff – constant interruptions and quite tiring treatment. But there is time to pray. I start early when they wake me with a blood test at 6am, say office of readings and then try to spend some time praying for hospital, St Mary's parish, people like Freda, yourself, your parish etc. Also of course all the family – people like Maggie and Jamie etc...

...Press on,

God bless,

Michael.

It was the last letter I received from him.

The previous month, Michael's cousin, Maggie Parham, had married his last 'convert', Jamie Fergusson, obituaries editor of *The Independent*, who Michael had received into the Church at St Mary's earlier in the summer. On October 19th, the evening of their wedding day, they had popped in on Michael in hospital before leaving for their honeymoon. Maggie later recounted how Michael had seemed momentarily non-plussed when they arrived; and how he had then explained that he had been praying so hard for them all day that when they actually appeared at his bedside, he wasn't at first sure whether they were in fact physically present, or whether this was part of his prayer.

In December, Michael was moved to the hospital of St John and St Elizabeth in St. John's Wood. Progress was very slow, testing that sometimes brittle patience. He confided to one friend that in his prayer he kept asking the Lord what on earth he was doing with him. Finally, he was well enough to be driven to Littlehampton, in Sussex, the scene of family holidays in his early childhood, to convalesce.

Michael arrived in St Francis nursing home on January 20th. An old friend from Soho days, Gerald Coleman, went to visit him the next day. While Gerald helped him to unpack, Michael, full of hope and enthusiasm once more, described all he had been through, his eyes lighting up as he was able to say, 'but it has been a wonderful time spiritually.'

Before lunch, Michael concelebrated Mass in the chapel from his wheelchair for the first time since he had been taken into hospital in October. Twice that afternoon, he said to Gerald, 'thank you for your long and faithful friendship', before asking him if he wanted to go to confession. Gerald, very aware he had gone to see Michael as a patient convalescing, nearly declined. Later he wrote:

> I'm glad I said 'Yes'…it was a confession I will never forget…that day was the day…when Michael said his last Mass and absolved his last penitent on earth. It happened to be me…his last words were 'Forget yourself – from now on just look at God, look at Him – all the time.'

That evening Michael's condition suddenly deteriorated; early the next morning he was rushed back by ambulance to London and St Mary's, Paddington. On Friday, January 24th, an emergency operation proved unsuccessful. Two days later, on Sunday, January 26th, Michael's left leg was amputated. He was still able to communicate on Monday and Tuesday when his close friend Anthony Baxter anointed him, but on Wednesday his condition worsened and he was moved into Intensive Care. That same day, he lost consciousness, never to regain it.

For the next three weeks, despite the limited access, Doris Fitzgerald (his housekeeper, to whom he had been especially devoted for many years),

Anthony Baxter, Astrid Sweetnam, Freda Berkeley and all those closest to him in the parish house and the parish, kept vigil, surrounding him with love and prayer. One of those who visited him, Catherine Goodman, was greatly struck by how strongly Michael's presence could be felt in the room throughout this time despite his comatose state. Eventually, he died on the morning of Friday, February 21st, with Anthony Baxter at his side.

The following week, I visited a wise old hermit – and friend of Michael's – Roland Walls, who lives in the Midlothian mining village of Roslin. As we reflected on the sufferings of the last eighteen months of Michael's life, physical, psychological and spiritual, Roland said that not only did it confirm for him 'the immense interest of God in Michael's destiny' and that some people begin their purgatory here on earth; but also that he believed these experiences 'were the final purgation of a soul whose mar-vellous ministry had in some small way still to be cleansed so as to be quite ready to enjoy the Beatific Vision.'

CHAPTER THIRTEEN

Farewell Father Hollings

The Tablet Notebook of 8th March 1997 began as follows:

IN A packed Westminster Cathedral on Friday of last week, there was not a seat left for Fr Michael Hollings's funeral Mass. Nor was it much different – though on a smaller scale – at the vigil Mass in his parish of St Mary of the Angels, Bayswater, west London, the preceding evening.

Black and white, the blind and the able-bodied, the nobility and the simple, they were all there in the cathedral. "You have from the highest to the lowest, because he loved them all", said one woman mourner, of Fr Hollings.

"It is very seldom that one priest should have touched so many", Cardinal Hume had begun the Thursday evening Mass at St Mary of the Angels. It was, in the words of Fr Anthony Baxter, "a bitter-sweet, sad-joyful occasion". The next morning, the truth of quite how many people's lives had been touched by this mere parish priest became evident. The seemingly endless procession of 129

Cartoon by Pugh

concelebrating priests and bishops (leaving aside the clergy who opted to remain in the congregation) required the organist to provide much instrumental fill-in before the final verse of the entrance hymn could be reached: "Changed from glory into glory, Till in heaven we take our place..."

178

The great cathedral crucifix hung over the coffin, which was adorned with a pall, a stole, a chalice and a book of the gospels, as the cardinal delivered his extraordinarily personal and moving homily: "Look, look at the crucifix and see there the Lord in agony", he began, and at the end the huge congregation burst into spontaneous applause.

When the long phalanx of priests and cardinal began to make its way down towards the piazza, there was barely a split second's pause before a woman slipped shyly in behind the family mourners. She was immediately followed by a mass movement, as the people of God followed with their bodies the priest they aspired to follow with their souls.

The Catholic nation had turned out in force to show what kind of priest strengthens faith, inspires hope and kindles charity. Michael Hollings was an ascetic with a reputation of having down-and-outs in every room at all hours. He may, in the words of Anthony Baxter, have been "short on deference", but "he opened windows and doors, and helped people to reach to the heart of things and breathe freely".

Text and cartoon reproduced by kind permission of The Tablet, the international Catholic weekly.

Fr. Anthony Baxter's Homily at the Vigil Requiem Mass at

St. Mary of the Angels
27 February 1997

For Michael Hollings

Speaking at a requiem I often start with words specially for those close to whoever's died. Today in the case of Fr Michael Hollings, a sense of 'He was closely, caringly, involved with me', will occur within a large proportion of you, as well as within many not present. You may have strong, mixed feelings. Relief that for Fr Michael's battlings with terrible illness are over. Grief and loss. Thankfulness to God for Michael's life. And so on. Michael himself would understand that mixture. If writing about it, he might produce a string of adjectives joined by hyphens, for a bitter-sweet-sad-joyful occasion. Above all, he'd stress – in tones more light than sombre (and certainly firm!) – that we should trust in God, pray, and press on.

After ordination in 1950 Fr Michael had six posts in turn: assistant at Soho, Westminster Cathedral, and London University Chaplaincy; Chaplain at Oxford University; and parish priest in Southall and then Bayswater. People within natural range of those posts tended to find he much influenced them. Moreover, he came to have a big place in the lives of vast numbers of further people throughout the country and across the world. That wider role grew primarily amid direct contact: through talks, retreats, services; through people spending a while in his household; through work on committees and social action; through his monthly letter to the sick; and through individuals streaming from all parts to speak to him – individuals with whom often he kept up warm links. Interwoven was his communication via TV, radio, and the print media: and his array of books on prayer and Christian life.

What was it about Michael that occasioned his impact on others? I can voice only a few, inadequate thoughts now. Many of you will have your own thoughts. You or I may well believe that in surveying the question just aired, one is pondering, in large measure, how Michael served as an instrument of God's gracious purposes in Christ.

In Michael's room, the window was generally open. (Incidentally, in Oxford, Southall and Bayswater he used one room for seeing people, writing, praying, and sleeping – on a sofa.) The window was open, and the door was open too unless for some special reason. When you went in, there was no fug, you could breathe easily. The room seemed crowded, amid a certain faded elegance to the furnishings: and the sign above the desk cheerfully said, 'Bless This Mess'. People tended to feel that this was part of their current world: not a world they could only enter once they were altogether tidily sorted out. In that way, they felt instantly at home, even if their sensations respecting the figure gazing smilingly, intently at them from the swivel chair might not be just chummy or casual.

People found that in religion and life overall, Michael opened windows and doors, and helped them to reach the heart of things and breathe freely. He took people where individually they were at, and sought to assist, urge them forwards. He never conveyed: 'If you want to get to God and fulfilment, it's best not to start from where you now are'! With his approach, people found they could both be themselves, and feel full Catholic Christians – not just bad and marginal, or outside. And they could give valuably to others without first needing to become golden successes themselves. Throughout, Michael led from among ordinary men and women: not from above or apart.

People saw Michael as taking basics of the Christian gospel at face value, and living them intensely, heroically. Over the centuries some such figures stand out. At the core of Michael's life and teaching was prayer, in many forms but with special stress on the more mentally still and relational (in effect, the contemplative). He had a pervasive sense of God's reality. He offered no general blueprint for how to proceed in prayer. But people realised he knew at first hand what he was talking about: and his ceaseless encouragement to others bore immense fruits.

Michael's preaching manner was strong, definite. He would proclaim firmly God's love and purpose for us, with few phrases like 'I think' or 'so it seems'. Some humans find a categoric style as such reassuring. Others may initially react with caution! Michael could indeed sometimes register a theme in its broad outline, undelayed by elaborate nuances. Across the extensive spectrum of personalities who encountered him, however, recognition recurred that so often as he preached, he was mediating the transcendent.

Along with that, individuals found Michael an attentive listener, free of stereotypes. His pithy, concrete advice, frequently delivered with humour, was so often seen to work. And the lengths to which he generously pushed himself in practical helpfulness were time after time experienced as breathtaking.

Michael had a tremendous sense of the scale of what was entrusted to him in care of others. To his eyes, this meshed with focus upon Jesus' phrase from the cross, *Sitio* – 'I thirst': a phrase on his ordination card, and his fortieth jubilee card, and now – no longer in black but in red – on his memorial card. Whoever in need turned up, from any background, Michael's impetus was to assist. Almost whatever plane the need was on, whether or not conventionally 'religious' or 'for priests', he was concerned. And he felt called to give urgent real aid: not just to cite sympathetically reasons (canonical or other) why he could do nothing. He was convinced that whatever your situation; however burdened or tangled by external circumstance or inner difficulty it might appear just now; there must under God be some positive way forward for you on this earth, so long as you have life at all. And why not, should you genuinely seek it, some positive future as a full, communion-receiving participant in the Church?

One can start to list groups for whom from the 1950s onward Michael sought to stand up within the social and church scene: blacks, those from religions other than his own, the divorced, homosexuals, men and women of the road, the physically or again mentally disabled, and so on. But soon here a notion of 'groups' becomes fuzzy: there have been successive individuals with their own circumstances and problems – one after another after another.

Michael's living by the convictions just remarked prompted some in Church circles over the years to view him as 'extreme' or 'unsafe'; rather short on deference, too much his own man. Images on occasion spread that his parish house was constant chaos, with down-and-outs in every room at all hours. (The reality there was not so, as careful-minded residents can attest. The former Guards major, the forceful, far from mute pastor, maintained broadly a good level of discriminating order. Of course, pressures genuinely present by no means suit each person's ministry.) Through the decades particular clerics may conceivably have been a little 'split' regarding Michael: for example, sending difficult cases to him, and expressing admiration; while for many other purposes seeing him as not to be followed. Pondering any such reactions to Michael, and their roots, lies open to us.

As to the way in which from early September 1995 Michael was for a while treated by certain journalists, and officials, I now make no comment.

Are the terms 'radical' or 'liberal' well used of Michael? They have often been applied. But they can mislead. His instincts were commonly to include more, rather than to cut out what was already there. He was not hooked on any large programme. Many of his words about, say, Jesus or the bible were fairly conservative. He meditated at length on church statements; and as a team player loyally backed numerous bishops' projects. Exposition, candles, incense, rosaries, blessings, were prominent. Enabling frequent mass and communion was a burning aim, whatever the cost to his own health.

Through the years many of us will have seen limitations to Michael, ways he could be difficult, and so on. Such features were often the flip side, the costs, of his strengths. Not all his efforts prospered. Today I neither veil nor dwell on those facets. It would be remarkable indeed to find a human being altogether free of some such facets.

Michael could come across as a person of polarities or contrasts. He was not over struck on some establishment ways in religion. Yet people sensed him to be at the core of and deeply loving of Catholic Christianity: by no means among those liable to shake the Church's dust from their feet. He was ascetic. Yet a constant supply of food (prepared often by himself) and drink, parties and good cheer, was central. He was intensely dedicated. Yet breeziness; impish, teasing humour; and deflation of pomposity abounded. I myself see him as at root markedly simple, trusting, without guile, and sensitive. He could be downcast. Yet for him God's love, eternal life, and the fittingness of hope, were – right to the end – unshakeable realities.

We pray today for Michael. But also we discern that his life broadly has opened a window through which we ourselves can be helped to approach those realities in which he – so one may think – now needs to hope no longer. Michael – we may trust – now shares in the crucified but risen Christ's triumph. There is much for which we can prayerfully give thanks and glory to God.

Cardinal Basil Hume's Homily at the Requiem Mass at

Westminster Cathedral
28 February 1997

For Michael Hollings

Look at the Crucifix and see there the Lord dying in agony, dying. Sometimes as you look, you will see how he is joined by a loved one, he too in agony, dying. On the Cross I know I see Christ, then the loved one. Sometimes on entering the ward, I saw Christ lying there, struggling for a life that was slowly ebbing away. When I saw you Michael, sick in bed, I thought of Christ in agony. Every time I glanced at the crucifix, I thought of you, agonising in pain, dying. It is a lonely business, dying, till we remember that God is everywhere and God is love. That makes all the difference. We can then pray with peace of mind what Christ prayed on the Cross, "into thy hands, Lord, I commend my spirit".

Few of us are called to suffer as you did, to make up – in that strange phrase of St. Paul's – whatever is wanting in the suffering of Christ. Not many of us are called as you were to undergo the agony of being publicly humiliated. It is good that it is the Lord alone who looks into our hearts and knows our secret struggles, how we have striven to be for him what all of us in our better moments would wish to be. You, Lord, judge us according to our deeds, you know what good we have done, you see the motives that drove us to serve you. You, Michael, were his servant and a good one. You served him, and remarkably so, in the poor and distressed, in those for whom no one else would care. Your door was always open for those who needed you, and your heart too.

You can look back, Michael, on your life with pride. Your war record would be the boast of any man; your care for students at London and Oxford put many of them in your debt; those you guided to the priesthood over the years learned from you what demands will be made on devoted and selfless priests and what joys can be discovered; the people of Southall and Bayswater had in you a leader who stood for what was decent and right in a multi-cultural and multi-faith society. The sharing of yourself in your many books reached persons who only knew you through your writing and were greatly helped and inspired. The simplicity of your lifestyle and the long hours of prayer gave you a remarkable pastoral zeal and spiritual energy.

Stop, stop – I hear you say – do not overstate my virtues or exaggerate my achievements. Do not give to others any excuse not to pray for me. I was as frail as any other human being, I hear you say. True, Michael, you had the weaknesses of your strengths, as we all do; yes, you had your faults and shortcomings. Who has not? In any case, you cannot ask me to list these here – *de mortuis nihil nisi bonum* (1) – even though it is fashionable in our day to try to cut down to size those who in life were bigger than themselves. We like, too, to belittle those with whom we do not

---

About the dead nothing except good.

agree. We can be very mean spirited. That is not for us today. So, Michael, I shall sing of your strengths, rejoice in the good that you did. Today we salute greatness in a man, we celebrate holiness in a priest, we admire a devoted shepherd. The rest I leave in the hands of God, the gentle judge of those who made Him their first concern. You did precisely that, Michael. You made God your first concern. We mourn you now. There will be tears in your family and amongst those to whom you meant so much. They will pray for you as you would wish. Now, as I look at the Crucifix, I see you passing from it to a new life, risen in Christ.

Cardinal G.B. Hume
ARCHBISHOP OF WESTMINSTER

Reproduced by kind permission of the late Cardinal Hume

BIBLIOGRAPHY
PREPARED BY JOAN COOLEY

A summary of the phenomenal media output of Michael Hollings, between 1948 and 1995, including television and radio, articles in newspapers and magazines, books and cassettes. This list does not include book reviews.

TELEVISION AND RADIO

DATE	TITLE	TV/RADIO STATION
1955 (8 Dec.)	Solemn Vespers for the Feast of the Immaculate Conception, from Westminster Cathedral (Introduction).	BBC Radio
1957 (11 Feb.)	Solemn Enthronement of Archbishop William Godfrey as Archbishop of Westminster. (Commentary). Also shown at Odeon, Leicester Square.	ATV
1957 (1 Dec.)	Dialogue Mass from St Thomas More Church, Eastcote, Pinner. (First televised version). (Commentary).	ATV
1958 (7 Feb.)	Sung Mass for Candlemas, from Corpus Christi Church, Maiden Lane. (Commentary).	ATV
1958 (21 Mar.)	Sung Mass from St Mary Magdalen's, Mortlake. (Commentary).	
1958 (1 Jun.)	National Pilgrimage to Lourdes, filmed for TV, produced by Michael Redington, with commentary by Michael Hollings, who had also been appointed Religious Adviser to ATV by Archbishop Godfrey. Wide coverage in Catholic Press, and whole page in *TV Times*.	ATV
1958 (Jul.)	"Christian Outlook". Discussion with Canon Mervyn Stockwood on the Encyclical *Miranda Prorsus*, re cinema, radio and TV.	Network 3 Radio

DATE	TITLE	TV/RADIO STATION
1958 (3 Aug.)	Children's Mass from St James' RC School, Burnt Oak, Middx. (First time not in church). Celebrant, with commentary by Fr Illtud Evans, OP	ATV
1958 (17 Aug.)	"About Religion". Discussion on Anglican, Free Church and Roman Catholic attitudes.	ATV
1958 (Sept.)	Evening Service from St Etheldreda's Church, Ely Place, London.	BBC Radio
1958 (27 Sept.)	"St Thérèse of Lisieux". Discussion between Gp.-Capt. Leonard Cheshire, VC, and Mgr. Vernon Johnson. (Introduction).	ATV
1958 (Oct.)	Mass and Catechism from St Joseph's & St Francis Xavier's, Richmond, Yorks. (Commentary).	ITV
1958 (Oct.)	Requiem Mass for Pope Pius XII, Westminster Cathedral (Commentary).	ITV
1958 (Nov.)	Remembrance Sunday broadcast from St David's Home for ex-Servicemen, Ealing. (Commentary)	ITV
1958 (Nov.)	"About Religion". 'Between Heaven and Hell': discussion with Sister St Helen.	ITV
1958 (Dec.)	Midnight Mass, from Brompton Oratory, London. (Commentary).	ITV
1959 (Mar.)	Dialogue Mass from St Mary's College, Strawberry Hill, Twickenham (Commentary).	ITV
1959 (13/17 Apr.)	The Epilogue (3-min. end-of-day talk)	ITV
1959 (17 May)	Pontifical Low Mass and Confirmation from St Thomas' School, Stanmore, Middx. (Commentary).	ATV
1959 (26 Jul.)	Mass from St Joseph's, Malden (Commentary) The Epilogue	ITV ITV
1959 (17/21 Aug.)	The Epilogue	AR-TV

DATE	TITLE	TV/RADIO STATION
1959 (12/16 Oct.)	The Epilogue	ITV
1959 (25 Oct.)	"The Question of Mary". Discussion with C of E Chaplain to St John's College, Oxford, and Dr Donald Soper, Methodist minister. (Over entire ITV network).	ATV
1959 (30/11-4/12)	The Epilogue	ITV
1960 (15-19 Feb.)	The Epilogue	ITV
1960 (Apr.)	Good Friday Liturgy, Westminster, Cathedral. (Commentary)	AR-TV
1960 (16-22 May)	The Epilogue	AR-TV
1960 (21 Aug.)	The Week's Good Cause. Appeal on behalf of Servite House.	Radio 4
1960 (25-29 Jul.)	The Epilogue	AR-TV
1960 (31/10-4/11)	The Epilogue	AR-TV
1960 ((30/11-4/12)	The Epilogue	AR-TV
1960 (22 Dec.)	The Epilogue	AR-TV
1961 (19 Feb.)	Evening Service from Oxford University	General Overseas Service
1961 (18 Jun.)	"Plea for Patrick" (Living Your Life series). Script by Christopher Hollis. 'Should St Patrick have been made a saint?' Dramatised version, narrated by MH.	ABC-TV
1961 (11-17 Dec.)	The Epilogue	ITV
1962 (14-18 May)	The Epilogue	AR-TV
1962 (10 Jun.) Whit Sunday	High Mass from Convent of Daughters of the Cross, Carshalton, Surrey. Sermon to schoolgirls. ("Broadcast of the Month" - Annunciation magazine.)	ATV
1962 (3-7 Dec.)	The Epilogue	AR-TV
1962 (11-15 Dec.)	The Epilogue	AR-TV

DATE	TITLE	TV/RADIO STATION
1963	YCW Mass from the French Church, Leicester Square. (Commentary)	ITV
1963 (25 Feb.)	Celebrant, Dialogue Mass from Oxford University Chaplaincy.	BBC Radio
1963 (18-22 Mar.)	The Epilogue	AR-TV
1963 (31 Mar.)	Celebrant and Preacher, Dialogue Mass, St Etheldreda's, Ely Place.	ATV
1963 (1-5 Jul.)	The Epilogue	AR-TV
1963 (20-24 Aug.)	The Epilogue	AR-TV
1963 (29 Sept.)	Commentator at Dialogue Mass from Chapel of St Vincent's Orthopaedic Hospital, Pinner, Middx.	ATV
1963 (14-18 Oct.)	The Epilogue. (Modern Parables).	AR-TV
1964 (2-6 Mar.)	Last Programme. (Special Lenten series). "God's Cross in our World".	AR-TV
1964 (12-16 Jul.)	Last Programme. "Why I Believe". Kenneth Harris asks for comments from AR-TV's religious advisers.	AR-TV
1964 (20-24 Jul.)	Last Programme. Conversations with Fr Borelli on the problems of human relationships.	AR-TV
1964 (12-18 ec.)	"I believe, but..." A series of discussions. Talks with Carlyle Schmidt, an Oxford undergraduate.	AR-TV
1965 (4 Jan- 5 Mar.)	Last Programme. 9-week series.	Rediffusion, London
1965 (Nov.)	About Prayer: Advent series.	Rediffusion, London
1966 (Dec.)	Last Programme. "Jesus – by John" (Week before Christmas).	Rediffusion, London
1967 (23 Mar.)	Good Friday: a Service of Unity from St Martin's-in-the-Fields, London. One of three preachers.	Rediffusion, London

DATE	TITLE	TV/RADIO STATION
1967 (29 Mar.)	Dialogue Mass from St Etheldreda's, Ely Place. (Celebrant and preacher).	ABC & ATV
1967 (June)	Religious adviser for series, "Sanctuary", about Convent life.	Rediffusion
1968-69 (Dec.-Jan.)	Last Programme: "The Other Side of the Coin".	Thames TV
1969 (Feb.)	"Padre Pio": film by Patrick O'Donovan. (Repeated on 1 April).	BBC2
1969 (18 May)	"Living a Lie". (How much do we conceal from people in order to keep their approval?) Clifford Hanley questions Kevin O'Dowd and Fr Michael Hollings.	BBC1
1969 (Jul.)	"Whom Do You Hate?"	Rediffusion
1969 (Sept.)	"The Question Why". Programme conducted by Malcolm Muggeridge with panel of priests to discuss celibacy.	BBC1
1973 (23 May)	"Sunday Half Hour", from St Anselm's Church, Southall.	Radio 2
1974 (24 Apr.)	"Churches are for People", from St Anselm's, Southall. Leonard Parkin talks to Fr Michael about community relations.	ITV
1975 (24-27 Mar.)	Holy Week. The Book of Kells – basis for series of meditations. 1. In the beginning. / 2. Incarnation. 3. Temptations of Jesus. / 4. Betrayal. 5. Crucifixion of Jesus. 6. He rose from the dead. / 7. The Resurrection.	ATV
1975 (29 May)	"Saints Alive". Magazine programme with Cardinal Suenens and others.	ATV
1975 (8 Jun.)	"Seeing and Believing" – Words, Stones & Silences. Martin Muncaster discusses three ways of praying. (From All Hallows by the Tower of London).	BBC

DATE	TITLE	TV/RADIO STATION
1975 (22 Jun.)	Mass from St Anselm's, Southall.	
1975 (Christmas Eve)	"Not Just Sundays" - the work of a parish priest in multi-national Southall. ("This is religion and religious TV, as this reviewer sees both, as they should be. Good and true." W. J. Igoe, The Universe.)	Thames TV
1976 (2 Jul.)	The London Programme. Asian demonstrations in Southall.	LWT
1976 (18-24 Oct.)	Closing programme. Michael Hollings reads one of his prayers.	ITV
1977 (27 Feb.)	'Sunday' programme. Discussing 'Living Priesthood'.	Radio 4
1977 (8 May)	"A Question of Faith".	Capital Radio
1977 (2 Sept.)	"Get Out and Push". Film about multi-racial parish in Southall. (repeat).	Thames TV
1977 (12 Sept.)	"Meeting Place" – Hope for the dying. From St Anselm's, Southall.	BBC1
1978 (15 Jul.)	"Man of Action". Fr Michael talks about his life, and introduces his favourite music. (Repeated in 1979).	Radio 3
1978 (13 Aug.)	The Funeral of the Pope (Paul VI). ("Excellent & unflawed commentary", *The Tablet*).	ITV
1980 (10 Jan.)	'Today'. Interview.	Radio 4
1980	Lenten Meditation, from Manchester Cathedral.	Granada TV
(24 Feb.)	1. Christ's Call	
(2 Mar.)	2. The Priest and the Burglar	
(9 Mar.)	3. Blessed are those who have not seen	
(16 Mar.)	4. Our Temptations	
(23 Mar.)	5. Our Failure and Guilt	
(30 Mar.)	6. Suffering and Death	
(6 Apr.)	7. Hope. (Easter)	

DATE	TITLE	TV/RADIO STATION
1980 (13 Jan.)	'Christianity Explored'. Ray Short talks to Fr Michael on the theme of "Hallowed be thy Name".	BBC1
1982	"Voices from the City". (Contributor) (Also in booklet published)	Thames TV
1983 (1 Feb.)	"City Priest". Thames TV visits Notting Hill ("an unconventional approach")	Thames TV
1983 (29/9-2/10)	"Night Thoughts". 1. St Vincent de Paul 2. St Wenceslas 3. Ss Michael & Angels 4. St Jerome 5. St Thérèse of Lisieux 6. Guardian Angels	Thames TV
(Sunday)	Credo: Confession 7. St Francis of Assisi	
1983 (18-20 Nov.)	"Night Thoughts". 1. Be still and know that I am God 2. Prayer is looking at God 3. Prayer is touching	Thames TV
1984 (11-14 Jun.)	"Night Thoughts". 1. I will never forget you 2. God first loved us 3. If you love me	Thames TV
1985 (Lent)	Prayer Matters. Lent Course 1985. "Confessing".	BBC Radio Kent
1985 (28/7-3/8)	"Night Thoughts" (with sign language)	Thames TV
1986 (16 Nov.)	"Sunday Comment", TV-AM	ITV

BOOKS

DATE	TITLE	PUBLISHER
1955	Hey, You!	Burns & Oates
1957	Purple Times	Burns & Oates
1964	Chaplaincraft	Clergy Review
1971	The One Who Listens (with Etta Gullick)	Mayhew/McCrimmon
1972	It's Me, O Lord - with Etta Gullick	Mayhew/McCrimmon
1972	Day by Day	Mayhew/McCrimmon
1973	Pastoral Care of the Homosexual (with St Thomas More Centre)	Mayhew/McCrimmon
1973	The Shade of His Hand (with Etta Gullick)	Mayhew/McCrimmon
1974	Restoring the Streets (with Ann Dummett)	Catholic Committee for Racial Justice
1975	You Must Be Joking, Lord	Mayhew/McCrimmon
1975	I Will Be There	Mowbrays
1976	Catholic Prayer Book	Mayhew/McCrimmon
1976	Morning and Night Prayers	Mayhew/McCrimmon
1976	Prayers for the Sick	Mayhew/McCrimmon
1976	Prayers of Love and Forgiveness	Mayhew/McCrimmon
1976	Alive to Death	Mayhew/McCrimmon
1977	Prayers for Others	Mayhew/McCrimmon
1977	A Wedding Prayerbook	Mayhew/McCrimmon

DATE	TITLE	PUBLISHER
1977	Living Priesthood	McCrimmons
1977	Spirit of the Living Lord (Confirmation)	McCrimmons
1978	His People's Way of Talking (with Madeleine Simon & Margaret Fittock)	McCrimmons
1979	As Was His Custom (with Etta Gullick)	McCrimmons
1981	St Thérèse of Lisieux	Collins
1982	Hearts not Garments	DLT
1982	Chaplet of Mary series – Joyful Mysteries – Sorrowful Mysteries – Glorious Mysteries	McCrimmons
1983	Path to Contemplation	McCrimmons
1984	Go in Peace	McCrimmons
1985	Christ Died at Notting Hill	Bible Reading Fellowship
1985	Prayers before and after Bereavement	McCrimmons
1985	Athirst for God (ed.)	DLT
1986	By Love Alone (ed.)	DLT
1986	Prayers for the Depressed	McCrimmons
1986	Lord, Teach Us to Pray	McCrimmons
1988	You Are Not Alone	McCrimmons
1991	Dying to Live	McCrimmons
1993	Love Heals	McCrimmons
1994	Praying with the New Catechism (Commentary)	McCrimmons

Date	Title	Publisher
1995	Reflections through the Church's Year – Year A	McCrimmons
1996	Reflections through the Church's Year – Year B	McCrimmons
1997	Reflections through the Church's Year – Year C	McCrimmons
1997	My Prayer Book	McCrimmons
1997	My Prayer Book for Communion	McCrimmons
1997	My Prayer Book for Confession	McCrimmons
1997	My Prayer Book for Confirmation	McCrimmons

SPOKEN WORD

1970	Counselling (record)	Mercier Press (Dublin)

TALK CASSETTES

1980	Learning to Pray	Bible Reading Fellowship
1981	Stations of the Cross (Narration)	Mayhew/McCrimmon
1981	Autumn Thoughts – (Prayer)	Mayhew/McCrimmon
1982	Chaplet of Mary x 3	Mayhew/McCrimmon
1983	Prayer	Mayhew/McCrimmon
1985	Listen and Pray (Gospel Meditations for 1985)	Diocese of Westminster Central Area
1986	Doing the Will of God (x 2)	Veritas (Dublin)

DATE	TITLE	PUBLISHER

VIDEO

1989	Dance to the Lord Pray through the Church's Year in dance and song	McCrimmons

ARTICLES

1948	An Act of Faith at the Piazza San Pietro in 1947	Beda Review
1950	Some notes on leadership	Beda Review

1951-1956	Meditations:	
	Prayer	-
	Poverty	-
	Patience	-
	Vocations	-
	Gentleness	-
	Christlike in Gentleness	-
	See the Lilies…	-
	Love of Our Father	-
	On Meditating	-
	Through Suffering to Glory	-
	The Precious Blood	-
	Holy Communion	-
	Mary, Mother of God	-
	Holy Communion – 1	-
	Holy Communion – 2	-
	Suffering and Holy Communion	-
	Suffering our Neighbours as Ourselves	-
	Who is my Neighbour?	-
	The Kingdom of God is within you	-
	Follow Me!	-

DATE	TITLE	SOURCE
	The Psalms: 1. Mercy 2. Humility 3. Faith and Hope 4. The Presence of God	The Saint of Lisieux (Lay Assoc. of St Thérèse)
1953	The Beda as I Knew It	Beda Review
1953	Every Year a Marian Year	The Tablet
1954	Athanasius and the Font	Grail Magazine
1954	Athanasius at the Bedside	Grail Magazine
1954	Athanasius and Holy Communion	Grail Magazine
1954	Athanasius and the Box	Grail Magazine
1954	Athanasius, Soldier of Christ	Grail Magazine
1954	Athanasius the Priest	Grail Magazine
1954	Athanasius and the Wedding Ring	Grail Magazine
1956	Methods of Meditation	Life of the Spirit
1956	The Approach to Non-Catholics 1. Ourselves 2. Common Ground	The Key
1956	The Cardinal's Grandson	Westminster Cathedral Chronicle
1956	The Symbol of Dedication	Westminster Cathedral Chronicle
1957	The Fulness of Lent	Westminster Cathedral Chronicle
1957	Abbé Pierre	Westminster Cathedral Chronicle

DATE	TITLE	SOURCE
1957	Newspaper Headlines of 1957	Catholic Herald
1957	From Good Friday to Easter Sunday	Catholic Herald
1957	The Missions and the Message of Lourdes	Catholic Herald
1958	A Public Examination of Conscience	Duckett's Register
1958	Cassino	Westminster Cathedral Chronicle
1959	At the Foot of the Cross: 1. Adam 2. The Two Thieves 3. Mary Magdalen 4. John 5. Two Absentees 6. The Mother of Jesus	The Tablet
1960	The English Dimension of the Church	The Old Palace
1960	Père Yves Nolet	The Old Palace
1960	Oxford Borstal Camps	The Tablet
1960	St. Teresa – October's Saint	Catholic Gazette
1961	The Common Ground We Share	The Old Palace
1961	Beaumont	The Tablet
1963	On Being With It	Roman Missal
1964	The Seminary and Prayer	Clergy Review
1969	On Being Alone	The Tablet
1969	Modern Blindness and the Hidden Signs of the Risen Christ	Catholic Herald
1971	Description of Work: everything under God	The Times
1971	The Need for Prayer Today	Catholic Gazette

Bibliography

DATE	TITLE	SOURCE
1971	Experience of Priesthood	Catholic Gazette
1972	Michael Hollings on Prayer	Christian Celebration
1972	The Reason a University Chaplain Must Be Seen – To Be Heard	Catholic Herald
1973	Bearing Witness	Catholic Gazette
1973	Witness to the Resurrection	Catholic Gazette
1973	The Witness of Mary	Catholic Gazette
1973	Freedom from Fear	Catholic Gazette
1973	Facing up to Reality with Christ	Catholic Herald
1973	An Approach to Parish Council elections	Christian Celebration
1974	Formation in the Parish: some tentative suggestions	The Way
1975	What Does the Parish Mean to You?	Catholic Fireside
1976	My Way of Prayer	Catholic Life
1977	Mission at Home: Non-Christians	The Outlook
1977	When God showed His hand and spoke a word of love – Jesus	Catholic Herald
1977	What I Mean When I Say Happy New Year	Catholic Herald
1978	Why Do I Believe?	Catholic Herald
1978	Called by Christ to be Perfect	Catholic Herald
1978	We Must Carve But One Hour a Week	Catholic Herald
1978	Following Christ through Suffering	Catholic Herald
1978	Why I Can't Do what Jesus Says	Catholic Herald
978	Greatness and Depth of Pentecost	Catholic Herald

DATE	TITLE	SOURCE
1978	Praying in a Parish	Intercom (Ireland)
1979	Prejudiced Nonsense!	Universe
1979	Liturgy Alive! 1. The Mass 2. Priest and People Alive 3. Church atmosphere 4. Reading and preaching 5. Silence is golden 6. Music and movement 7. Sharing the Eucharistic – Prayer and Communion 8. Go, the Mass is ended	Catholic Herald
1980	Don't Let Charity Stay At Home	TV Times
1980	How Jesus Would Have Seen Off Parky & Co.	TV Times
1982	A Stepping Stone to Our Lord	Catholic Herald
1983	No Room at the Inn	The Tablet
1984	The Untidiness of God	The Tablet
1984	Purgatory: a place of hope	Universe
1984	The Fact of Life	The Tablet
1984	The Living Spirit	The Tablet
1985	Viewpoint: Dust and Diamond	The Tablet
1985	Musings on Late Vocations	Beda Review (Jubilee)
1985	Come Lord Jesus 1. Lord, teach us to pray 2. Taking God seriously 3. The need for silence 4. The growth of the group	Universe

DATE	TITLE	SOURCE
1985	Whose Hand on the Schools Tiller?	Catholic Herald
1985	Jolts from God?	Universe
1986	Apartheid in the Church?	The Tablet
1986	The Life of the Priest – what is special?	The Mulberry
1987	Drugs War Matters to Us All	Westminster Record
1988	Bless this Mess	The Tablet
1988	Love is All You Need	Universe
1988	Teach Yourself to Pray	The Sower
1993	Deepening our Spiritual Life	Priests & People
1993	An Open Door	'Africa'
1994	Faith, Hope and Joy in Lourdes	Universe
1994	Praying Our Way through Lent	Catholic Times
1994	Seventy Times Seven	The Tablet
1994	Vocations (We must all find our own way to live)	Universe
1995	The Lourdes effect	The Tablet

Acknowledgements

I would like to express my gratitude to all who helped in any way in the evolution of the book's first three chapters – about Michael's formative years – and the last chapter, about the final months of Michael's life and his Way of the Cross.

Joan Cooley, Alasdair Black and Henrietta Phipps who originally formed the 'Fr Michael Appeal Book Sub-Committee' and who then generously handed on their research, including the interview with Fr Ronald Moffat, SJ and the reminiscences of Ian Fraser and Gerald Coleman.
Joan, in addition, continued to hunt out and send on much other valuable information – and to offer warm encouragement and prayerful support.

Tony and Jennifer Hollings, Michael's brother and sister-in-law, Sylvia his sister, Elsie Gibbs his cousin, Edward Corbould, the younger brother of his close friend, John Corbould, and all who offered first hand information about the first twenty-eight years of Michael's life.

Freda Berkeley, Anthony Baxter, Catherine Goodman, Maggie and Jamie Fergusson and all who shed further light on the last eighteen months of his life.

Many of the above, my parents, Hew and Anne-Louise Dalrymple, my brother William, Alice Littlewood, Jane Miezitis, Marguerite Kramers, Bernard Traynor, Nicholas Hudson, Roland Walls, Alberic Stackpoole, Alexander Sherbrooke and Rags Hay-Will and especially my fellow editors, Joan and Terry – all who commented helpfully on the chapters at different stages in their creation.

And finally, Una Johnston, the most indefatigable, patient and generous of typists, and Grace Lee, still a supreme photocopier and much more, who ensured these chapters actually saw the light of day.

To end on a personal note; seven hours after Michael died at 1.50am on February 21st, 1997, there was born in the same hospital, St Mary's, Paddington, his first cousin, twice removed, Samuel Dalrymple – also great nephew of Fr Jock Dalrymple (senior), and my nephew and godson.

Jock Dalrymple